Flowery Dreams

A Kawaii Coloring Book of Flowers and Chibis by YamPuff

Copyright © 2020 Yasmeen Eldahan, All rights reserved
yampuff.com

Cover and book design by Yasmeen Eldahan

ISBN: 9798620264063

This book is for personal, non-commercial use only. While you are welcome to share pictures of this book and your coloring online, you may not take pictures, copies or scans of blank (uncolored) pages to sell or give away without prior consent from the author. When sharing online, please credit me, with a link to my page and/or with the hashtag #YAMPUFF

Thank you!

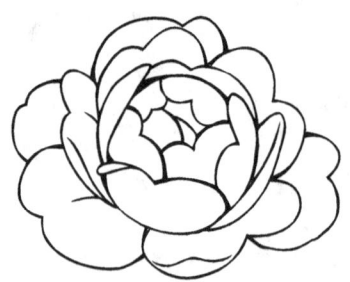

Welcome to my latest coloring book.
I hope you enjoy it!
—YamPuff

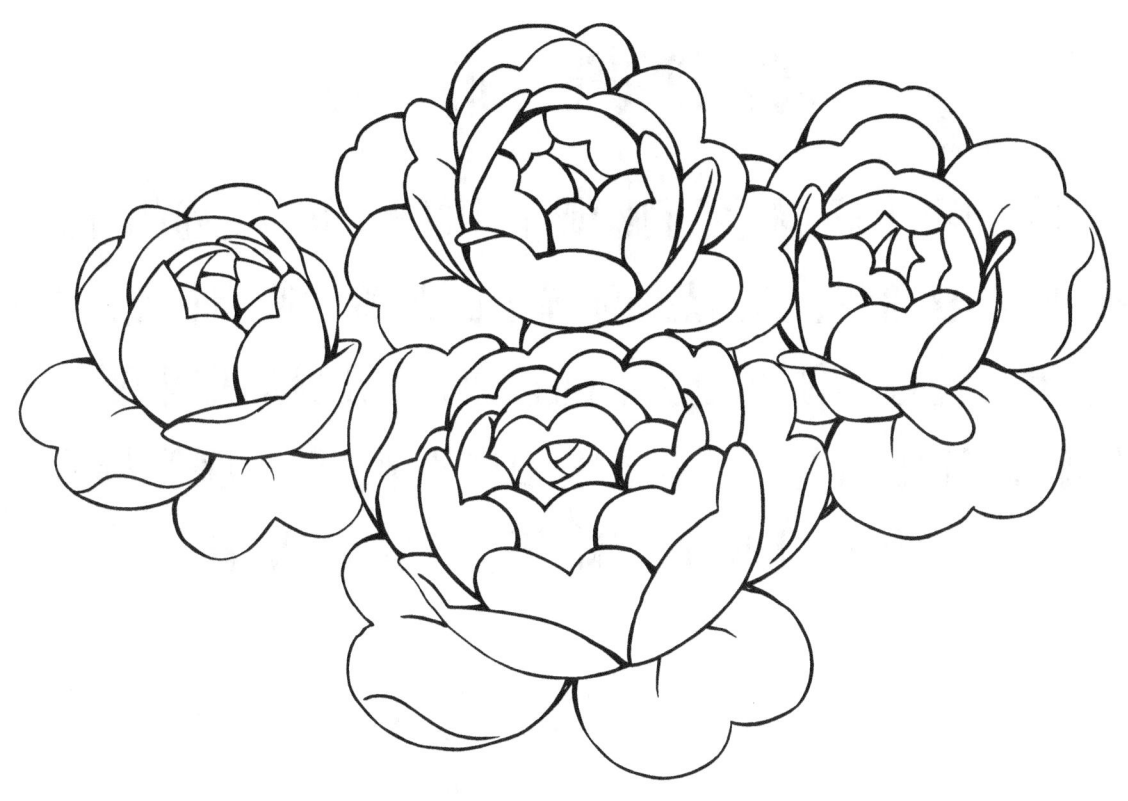

Check out

YAMPUFF.COM

For contests, free coloring pages (digital stamps), coloring book updates, tips, tricks, and more!

How to Use This Book:

When coloring, I recommend for you to place a thick and/or bleedproof piece of paper behind the page you are coloring. This wil prevent any color from leaking onto subsequent pages and also save them from getting any dents or marks. Crayons, gel pens, colored pencils alcohol-based markers, regular markers, and more, will all work!

Happy coloring!
-YamPuff

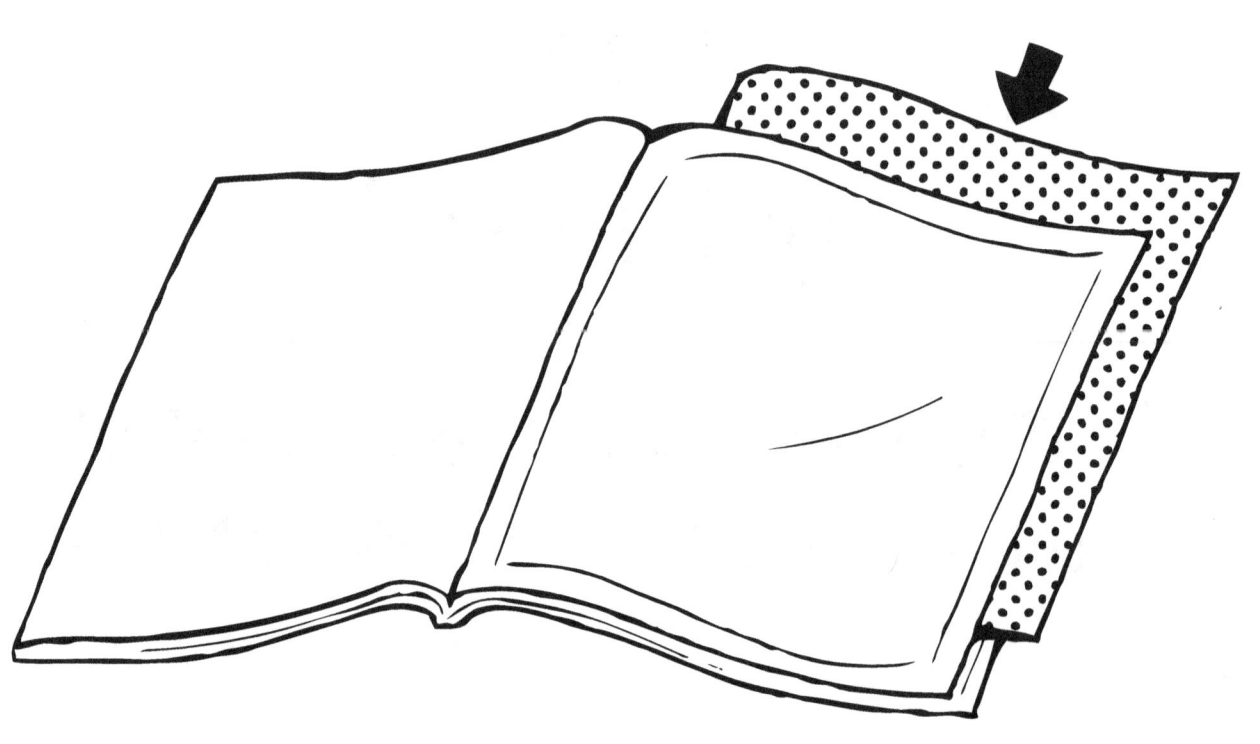

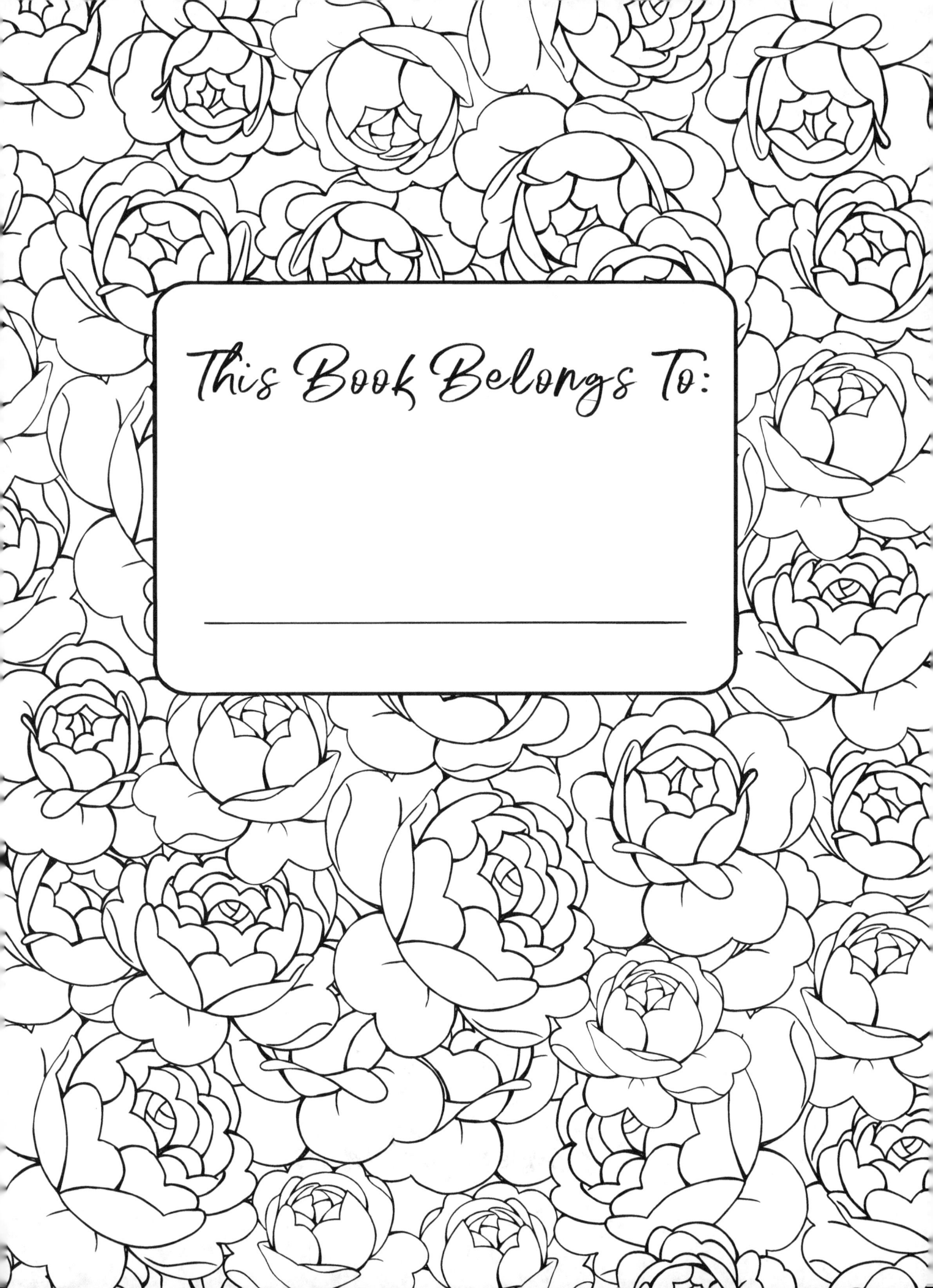

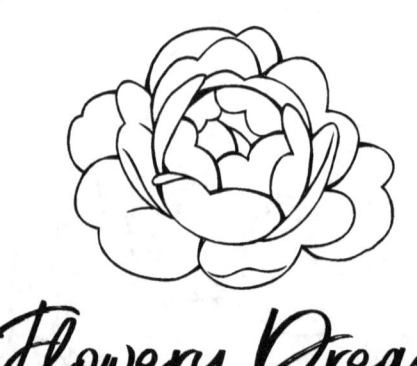

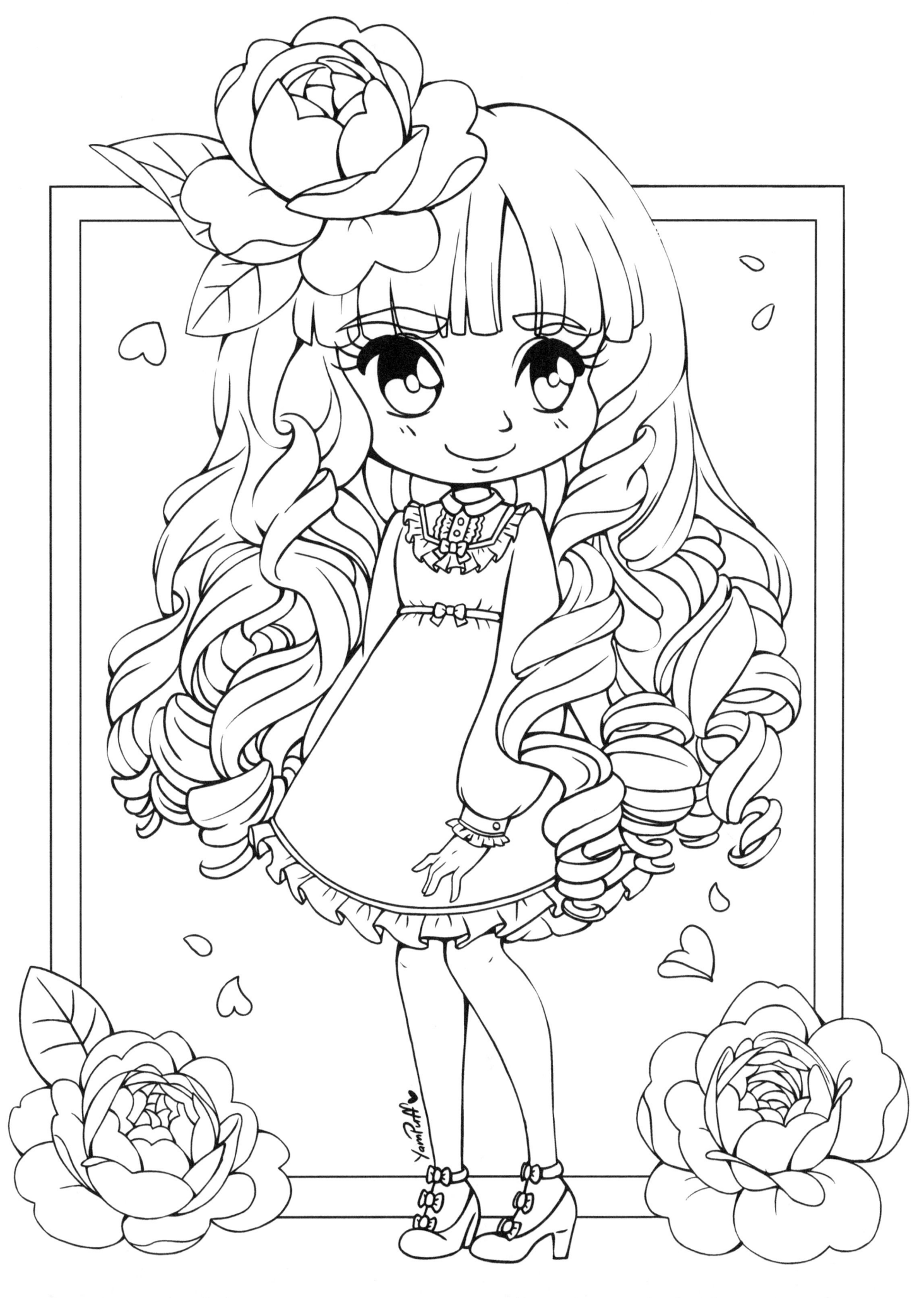

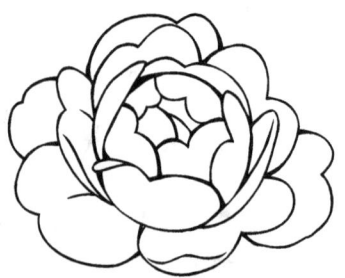

Roses

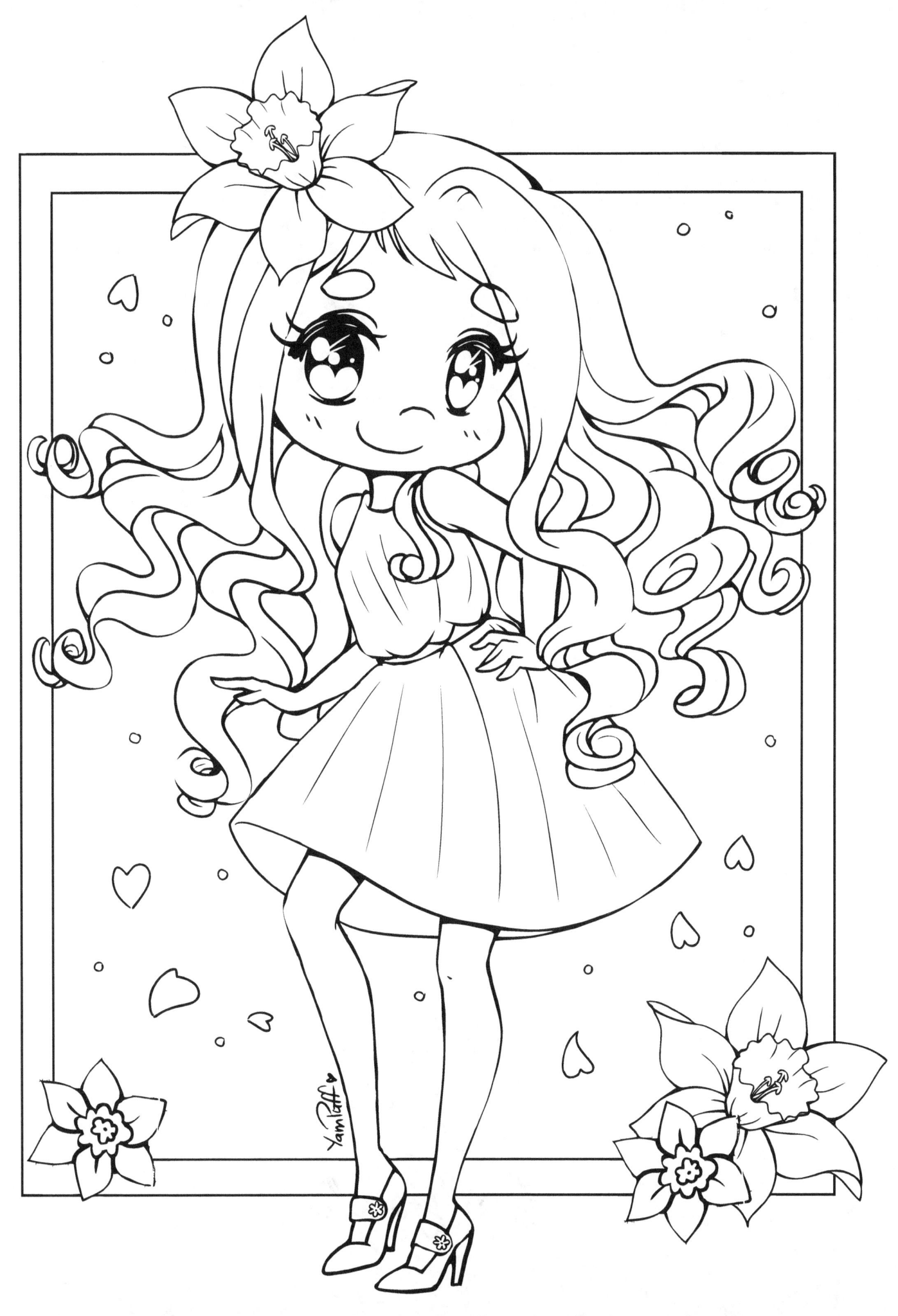

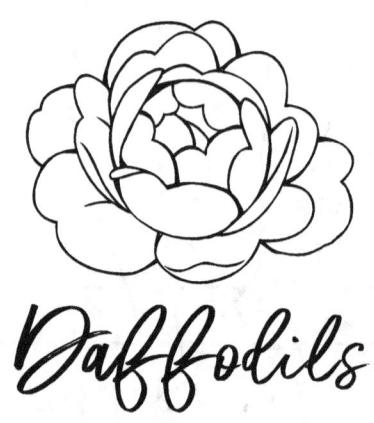

Daffodils

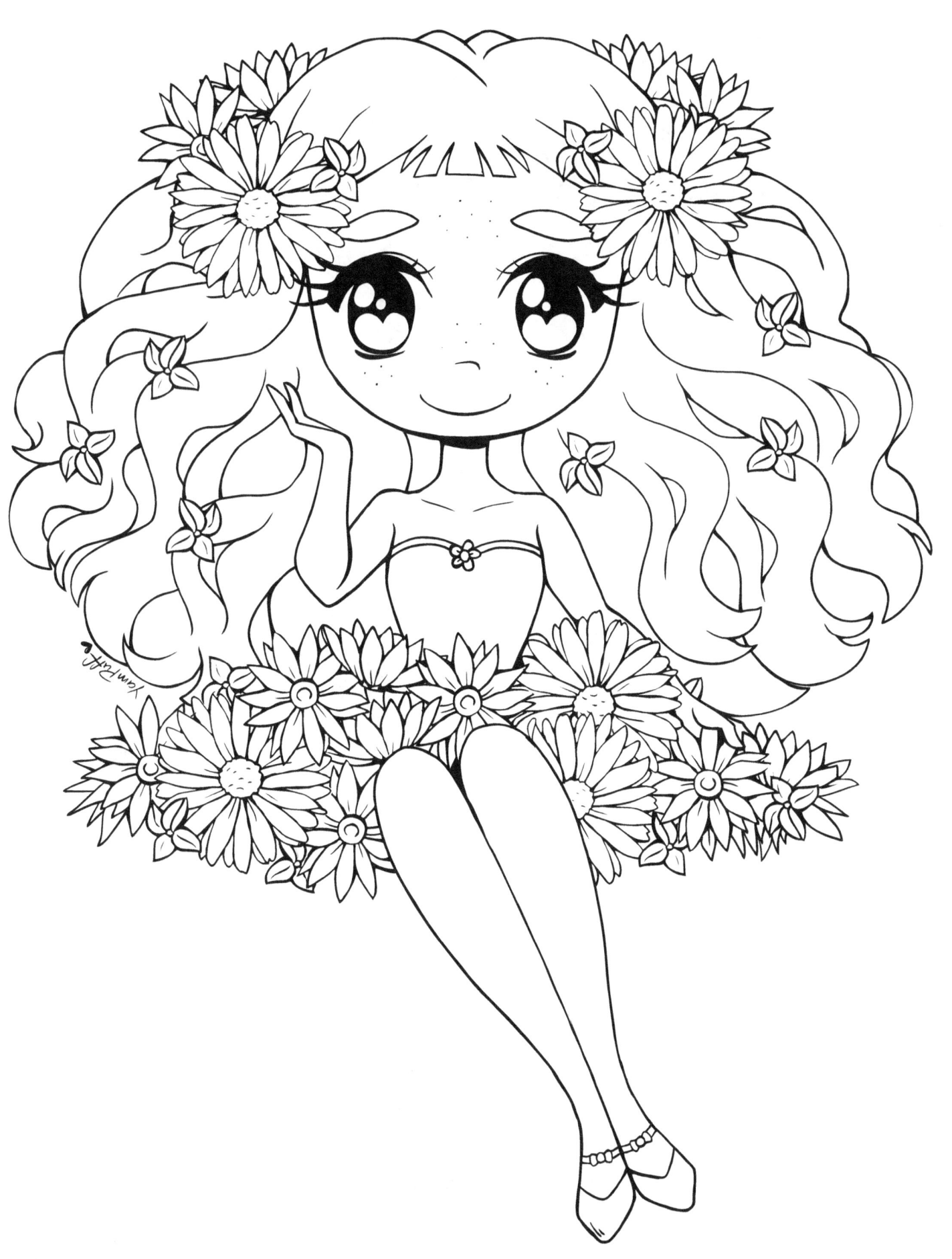

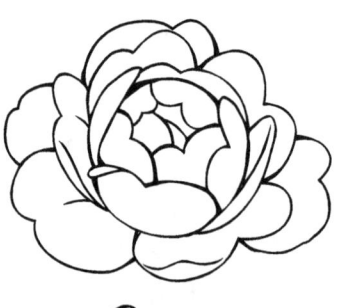

Asters

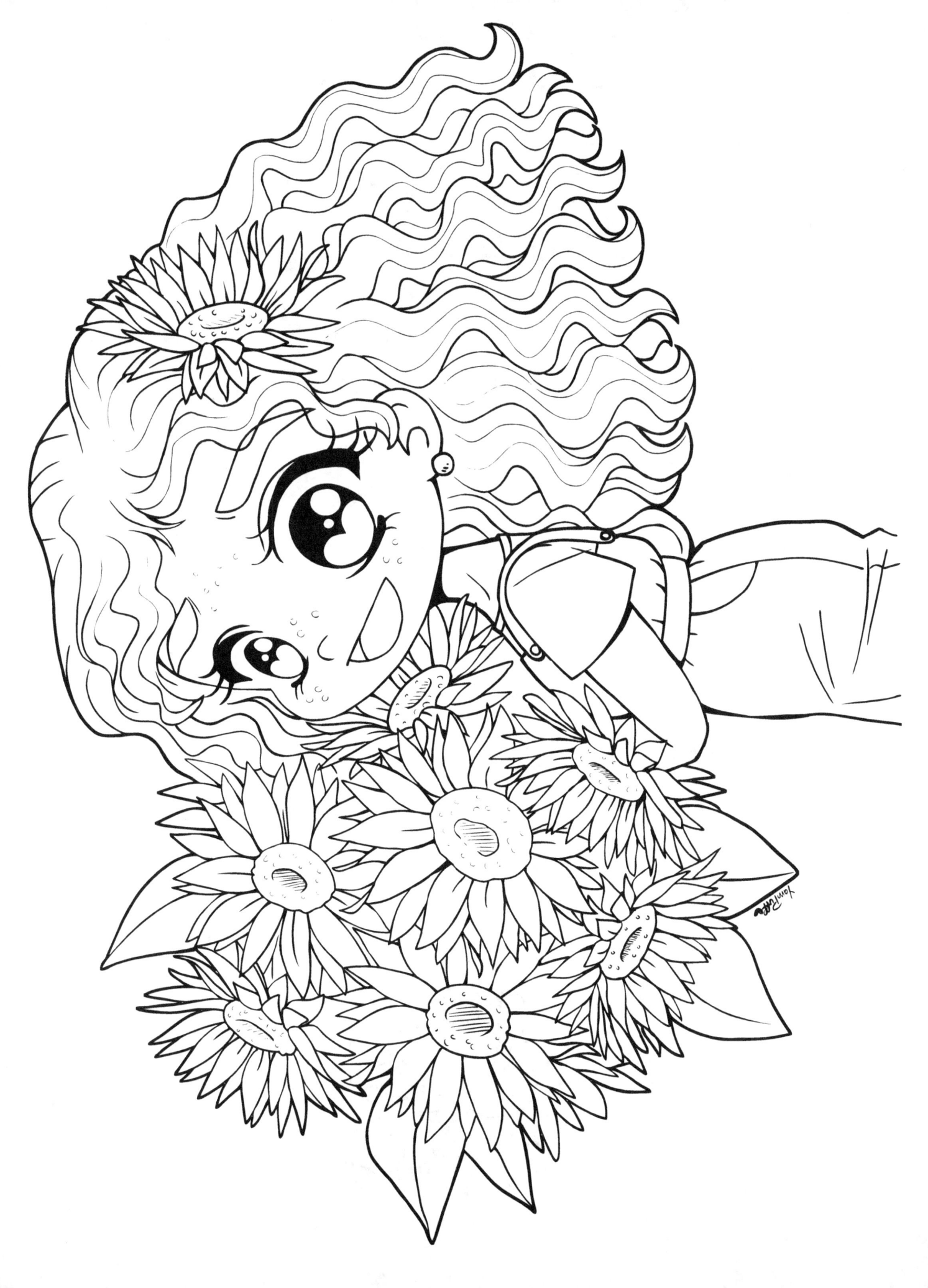

Sunflowers

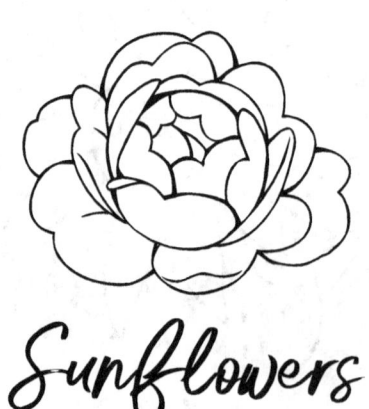

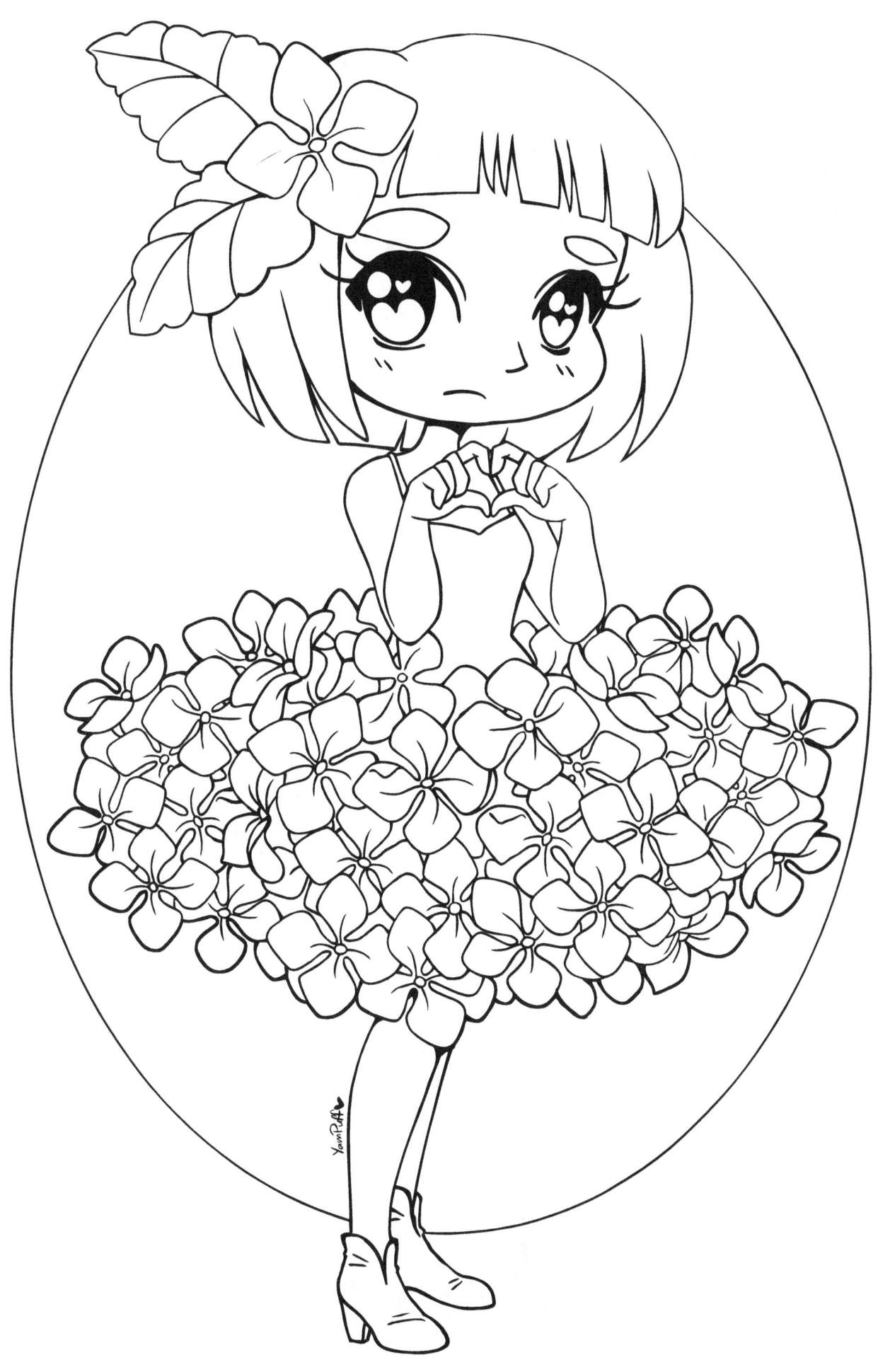

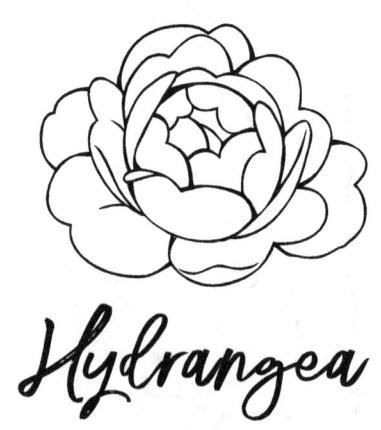

Hydrangea

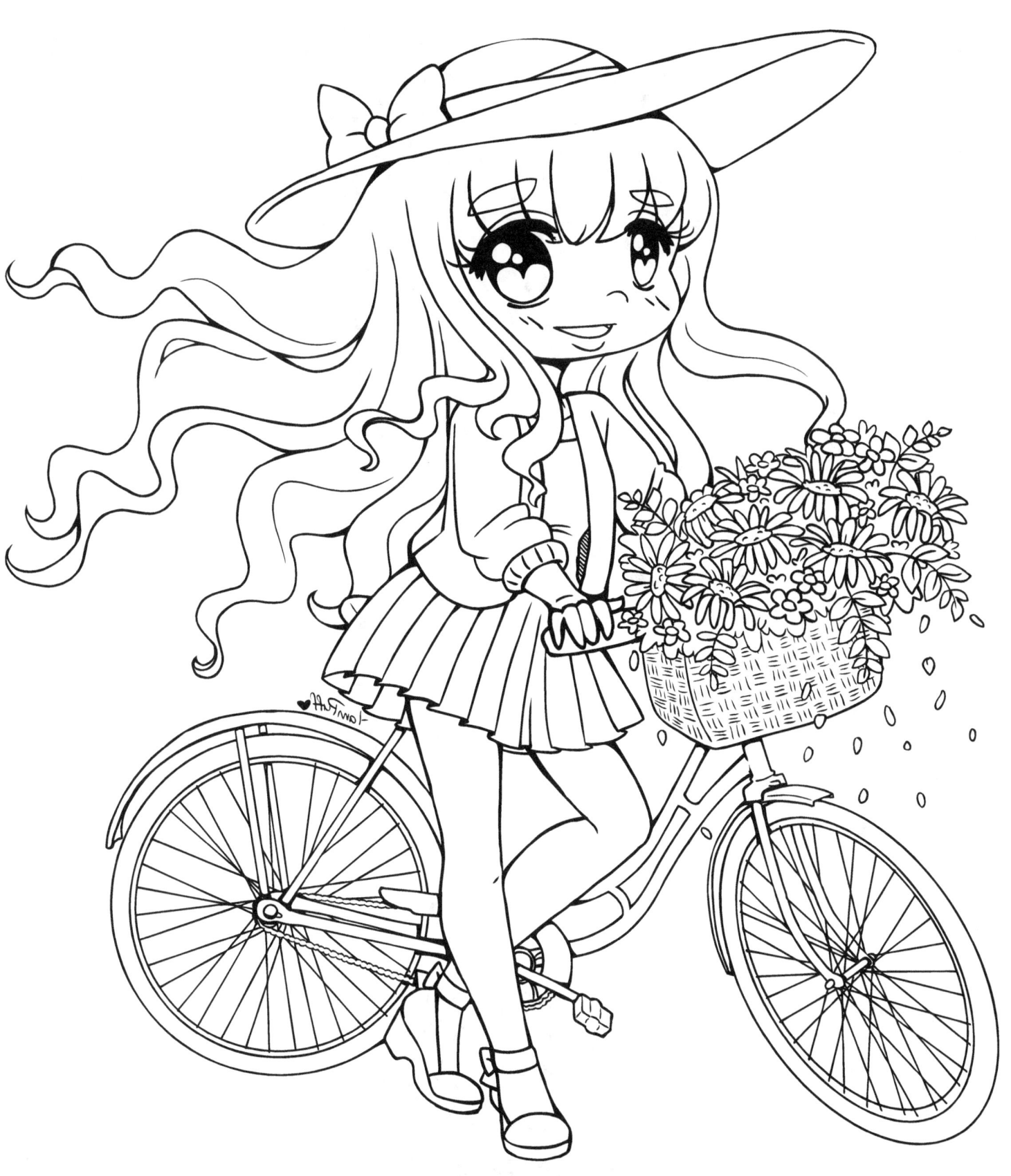

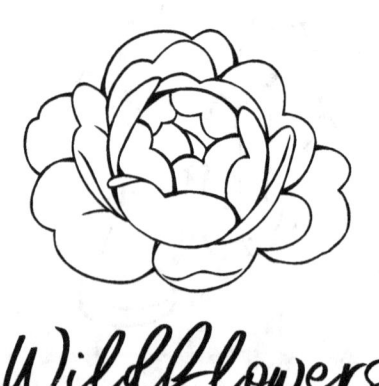

Wildflowers

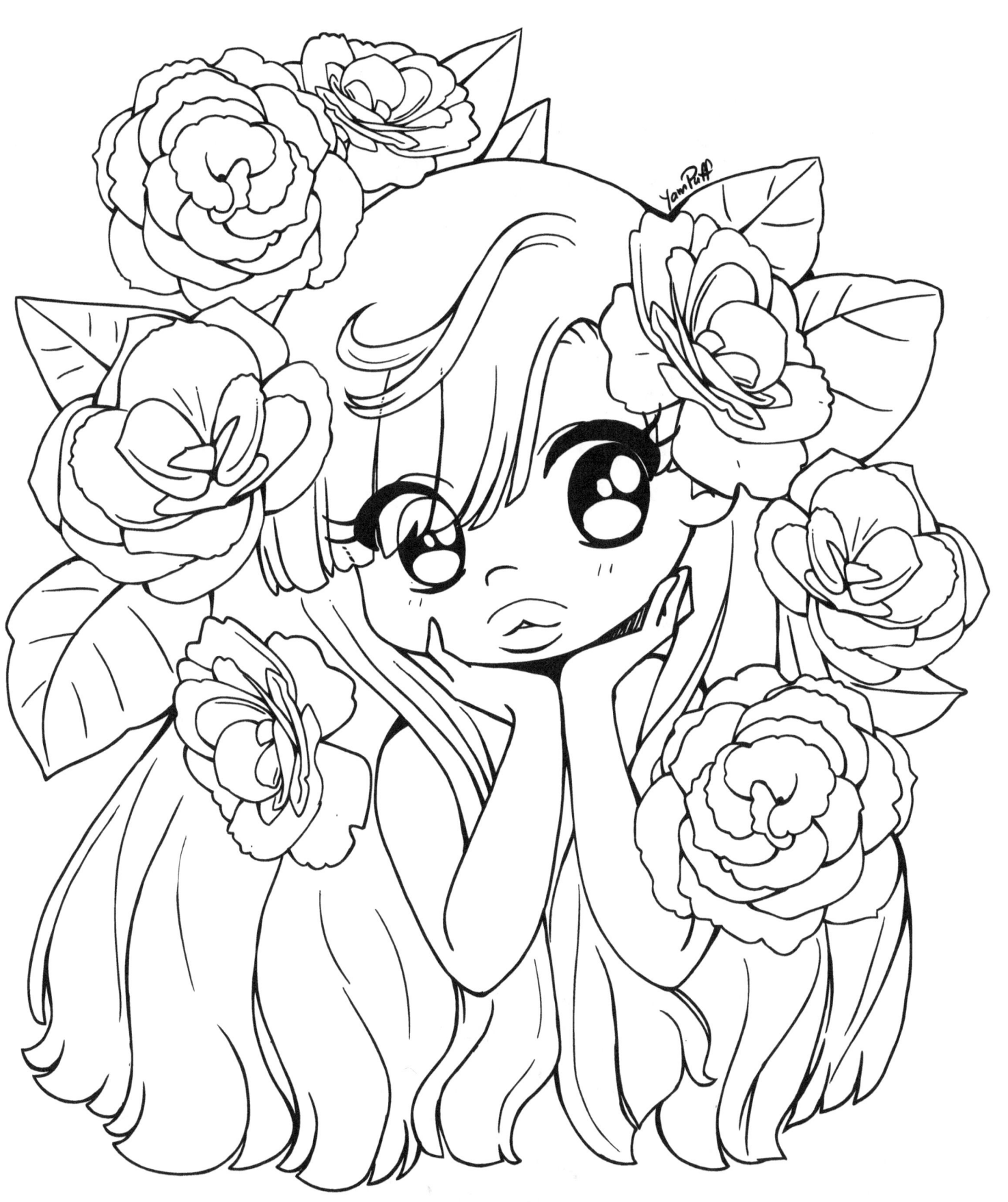

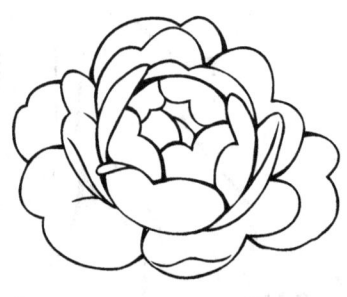
Peonies

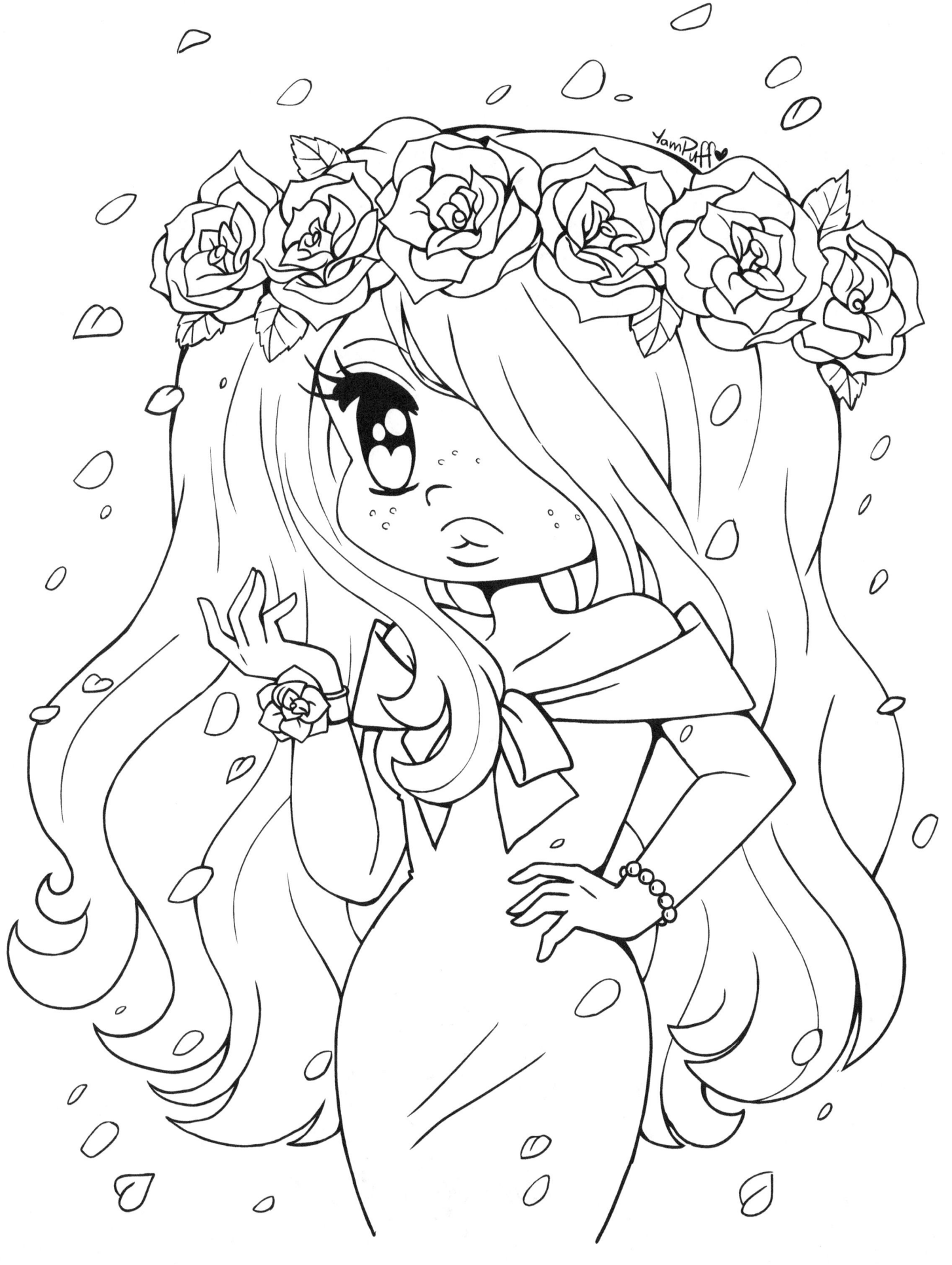

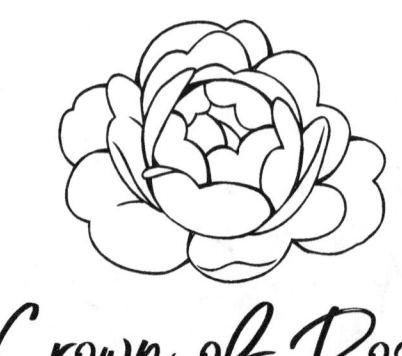

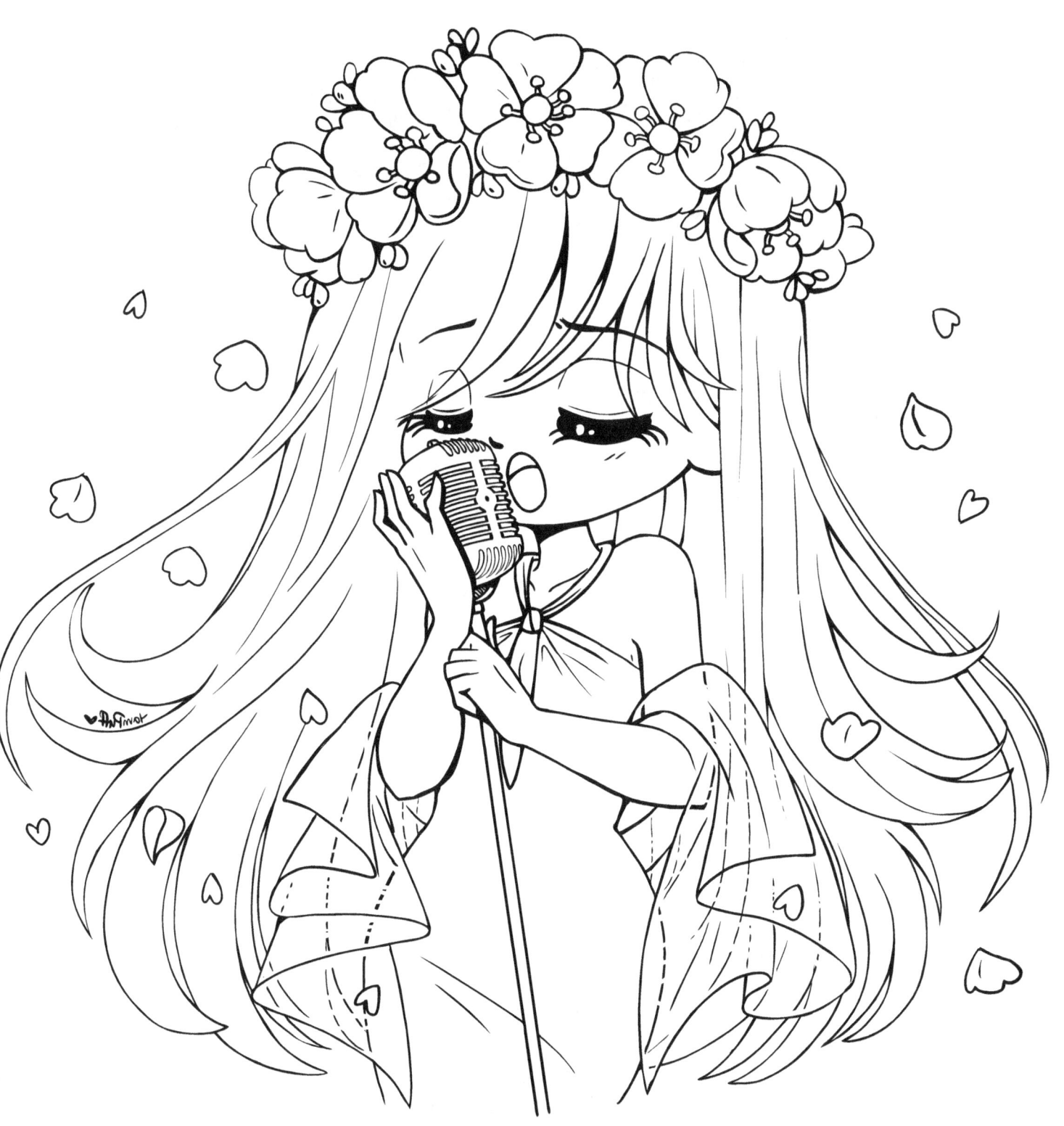

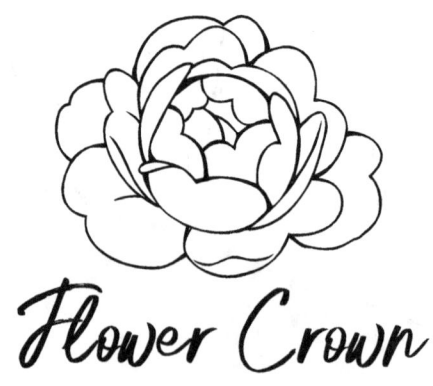

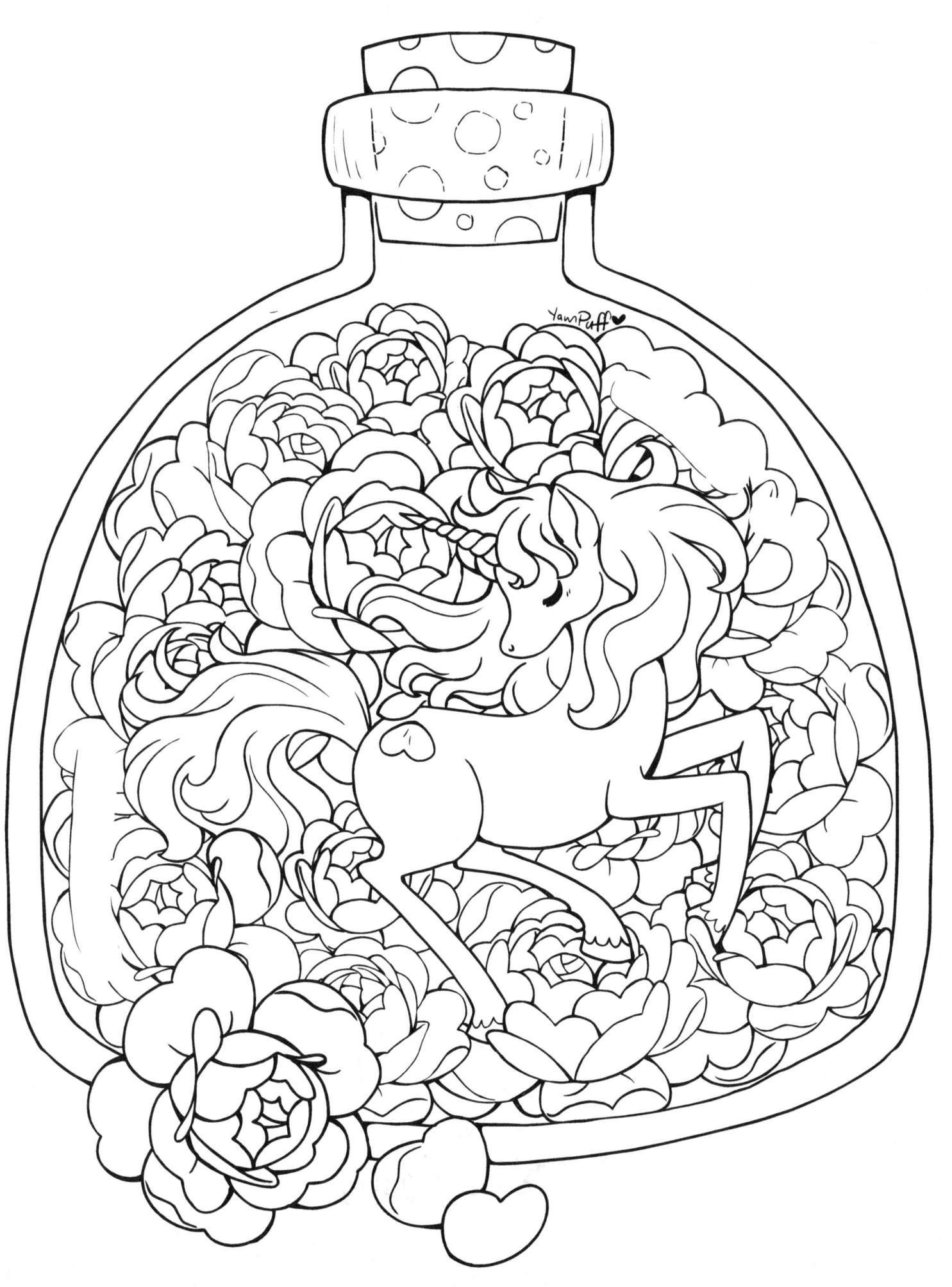

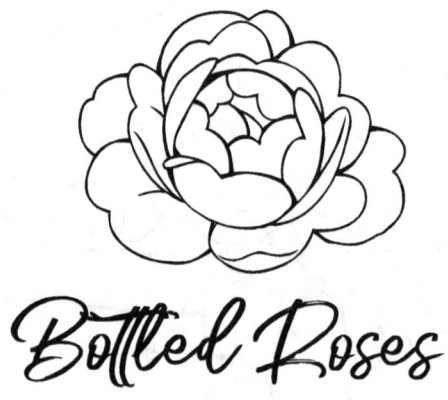

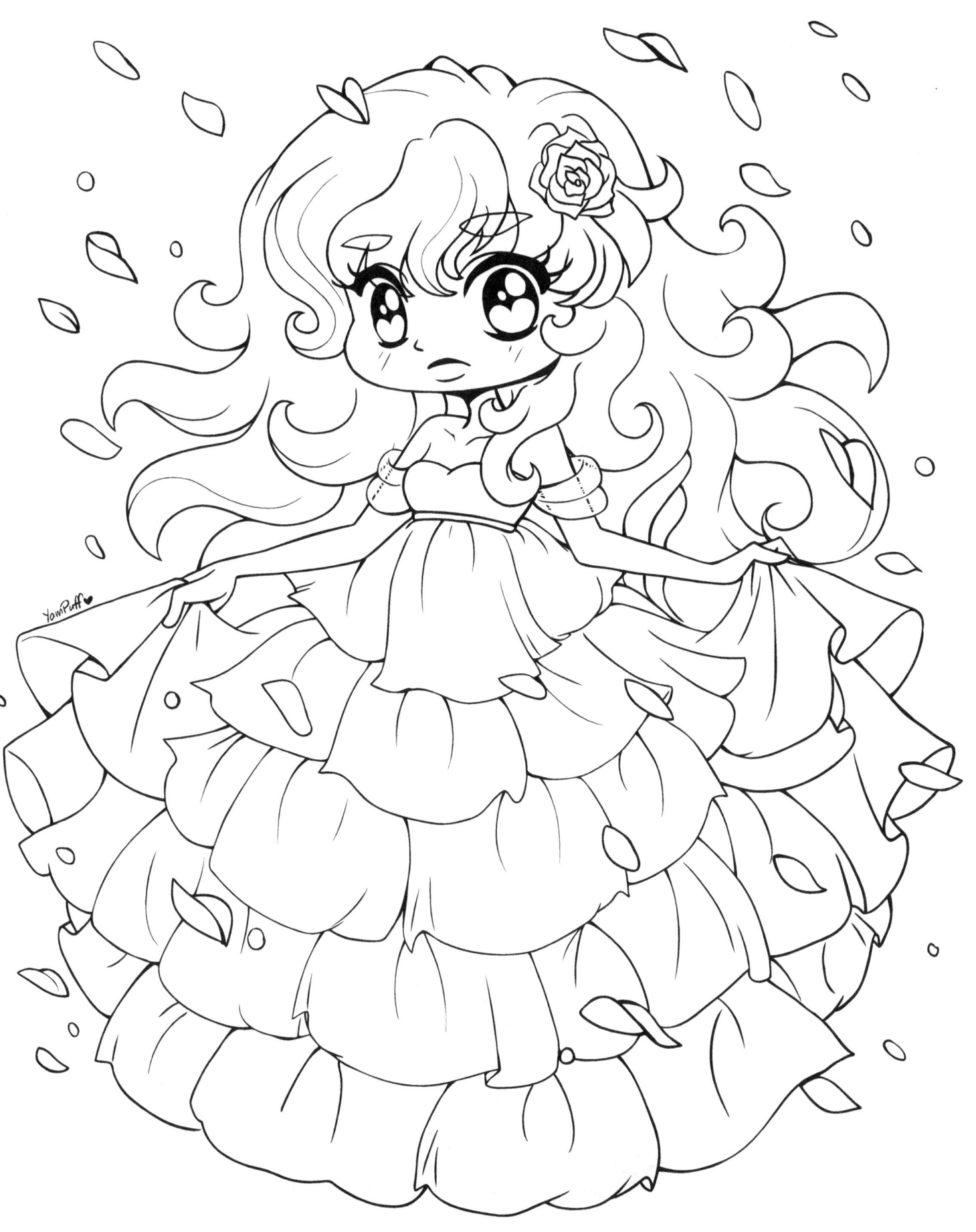

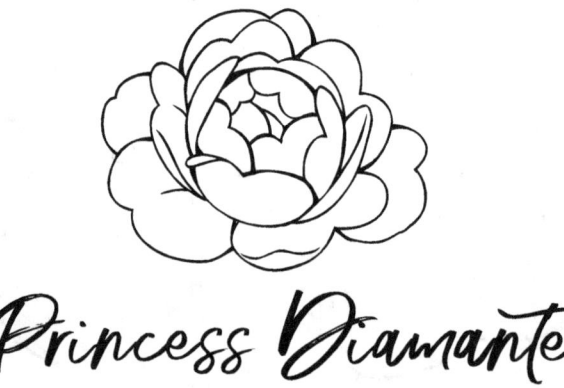

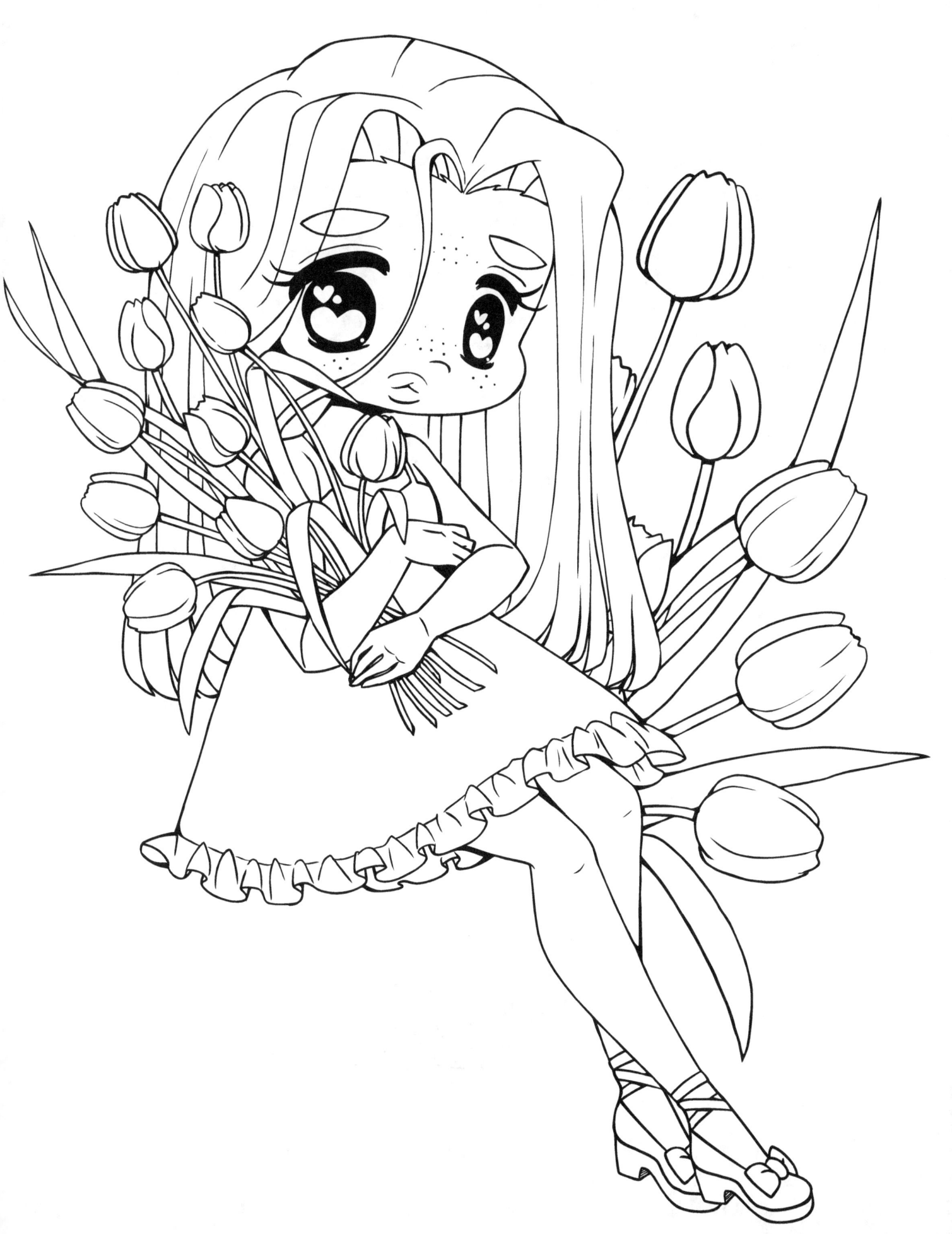

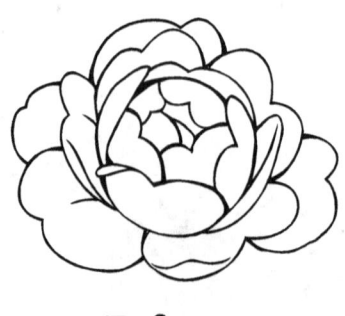

Tulips

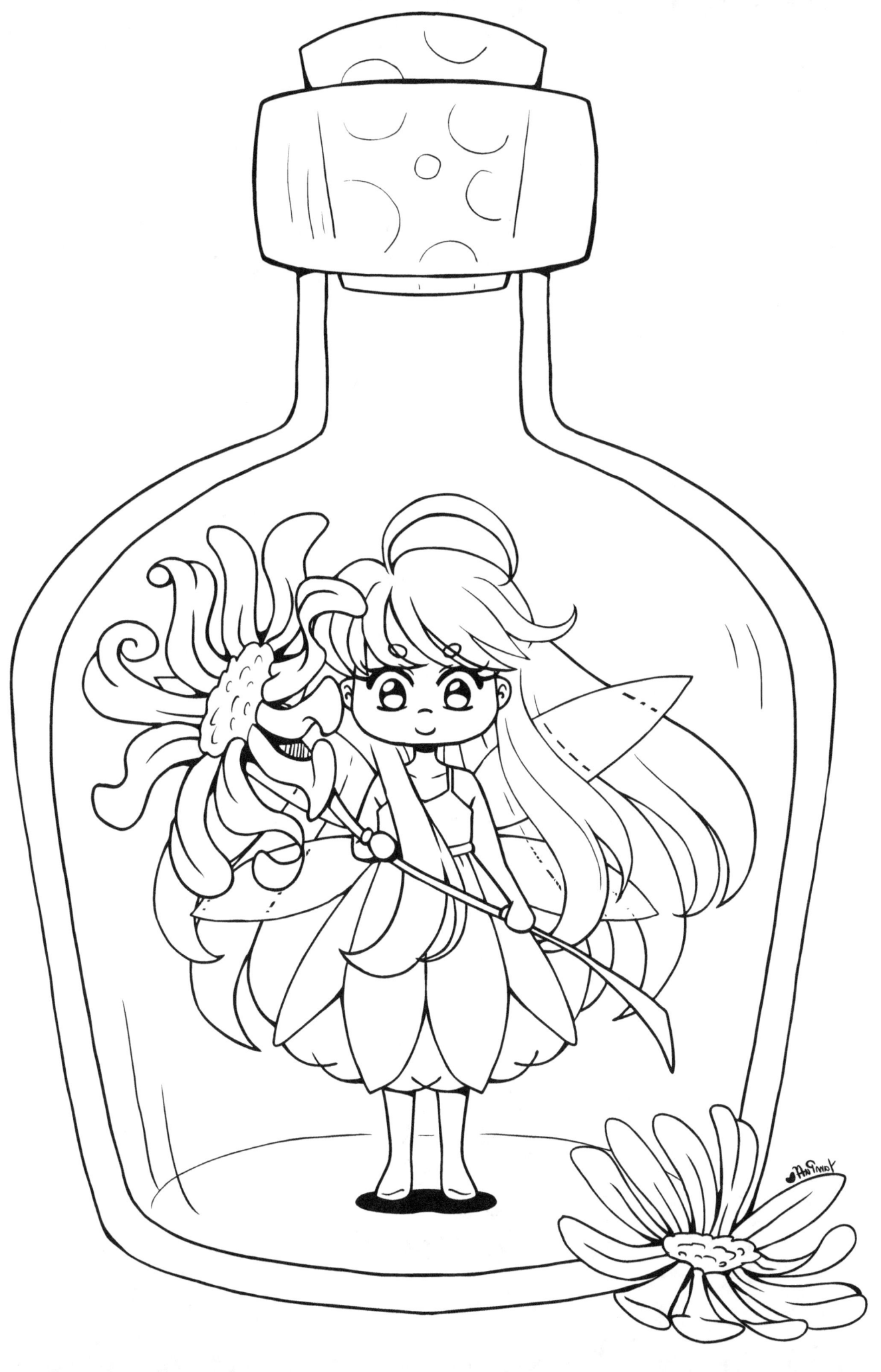

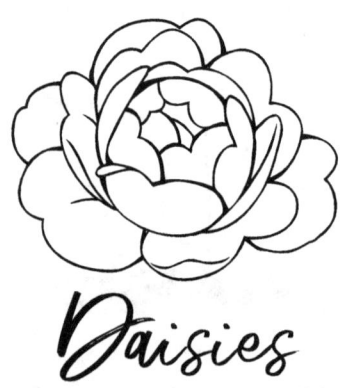

Daisies

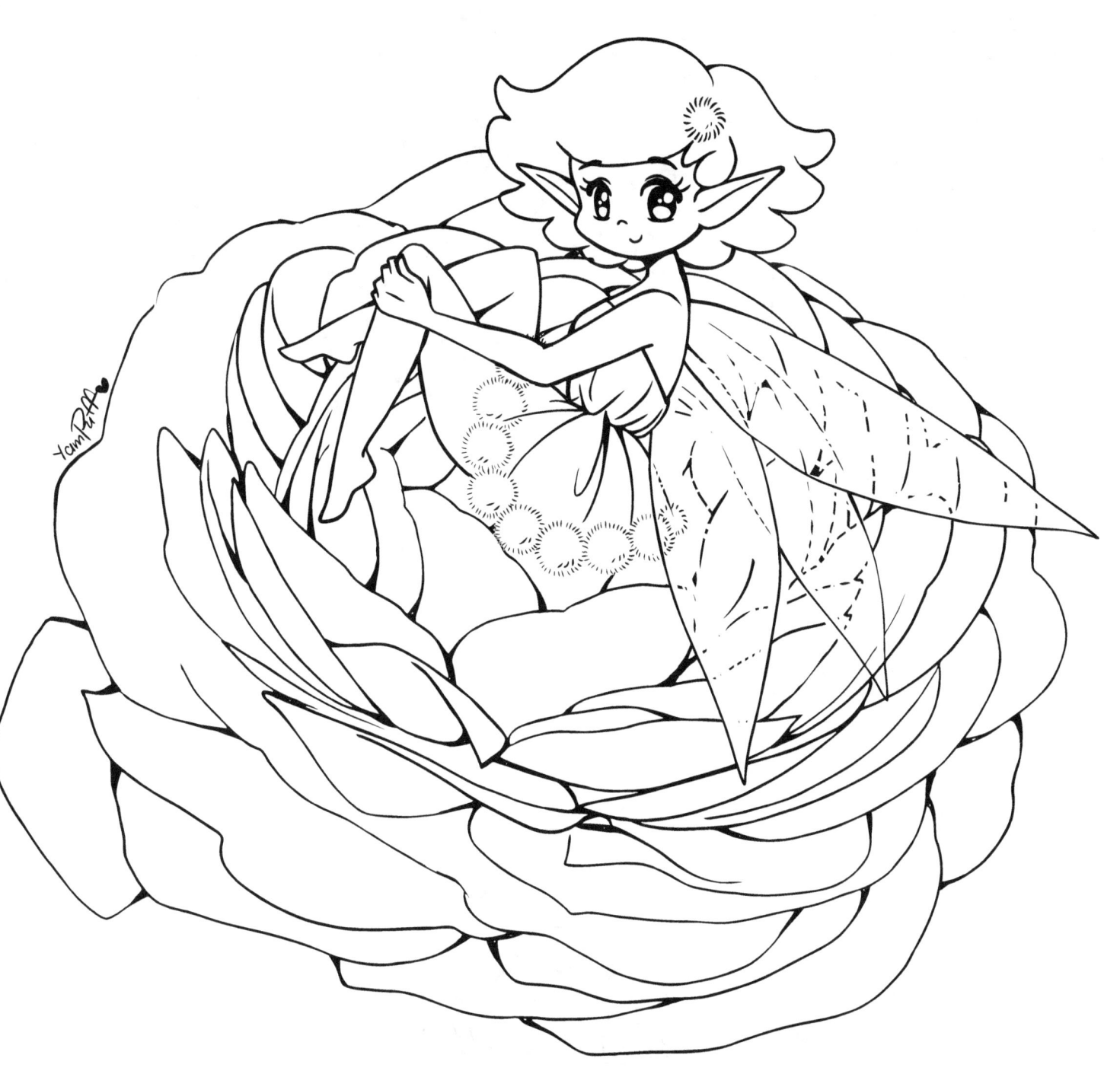

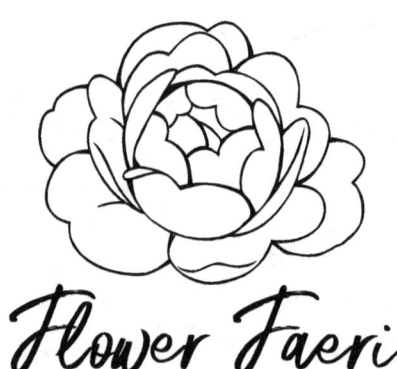

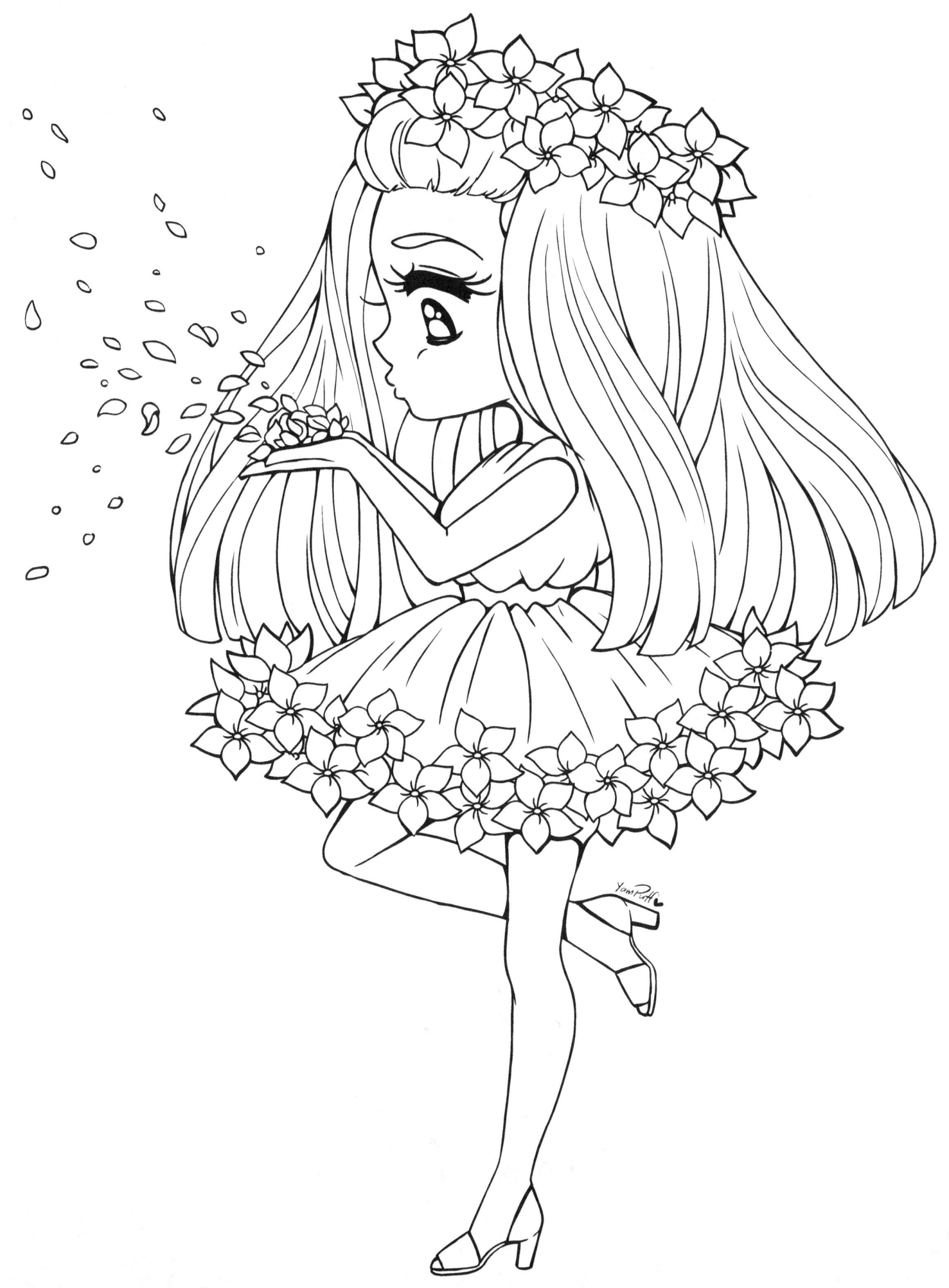

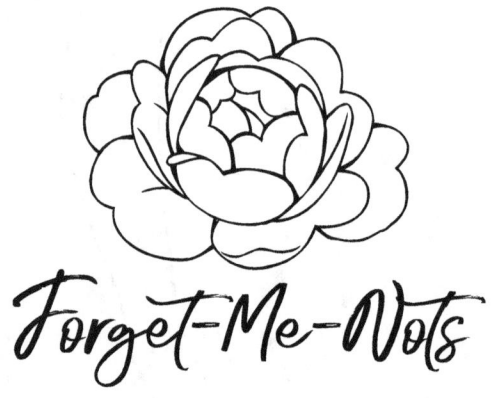

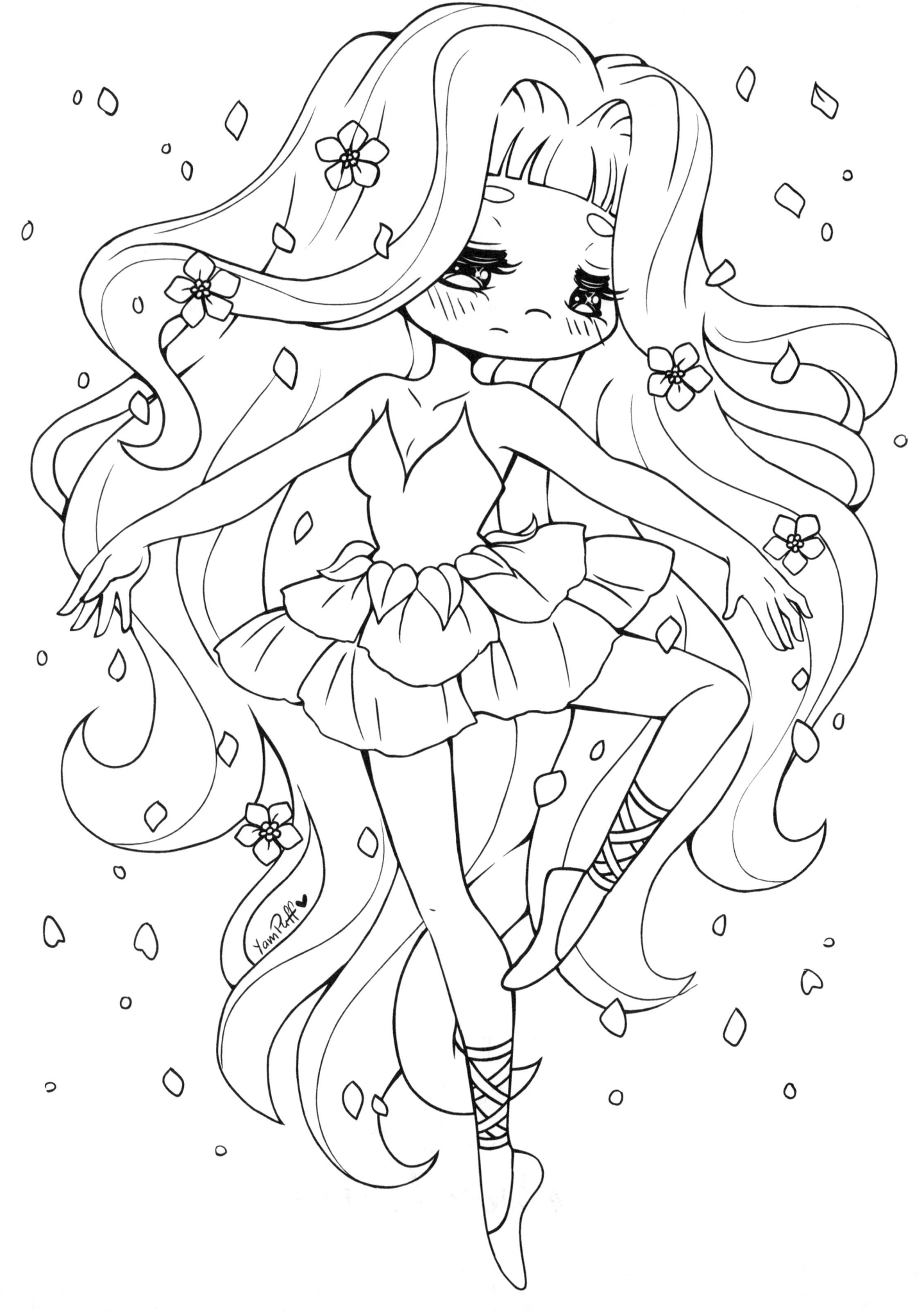

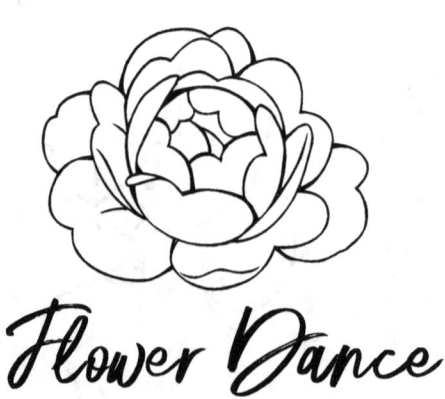

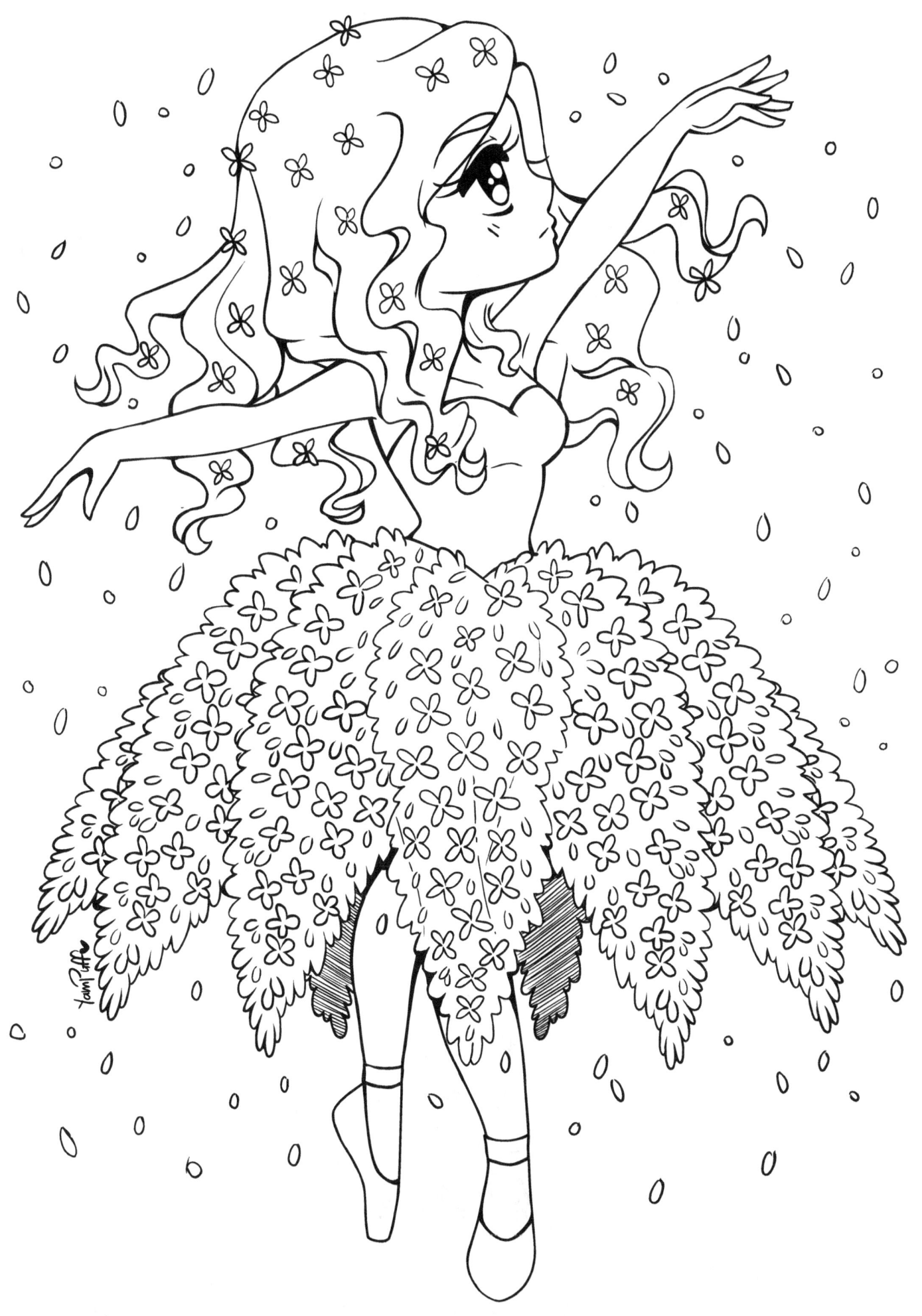

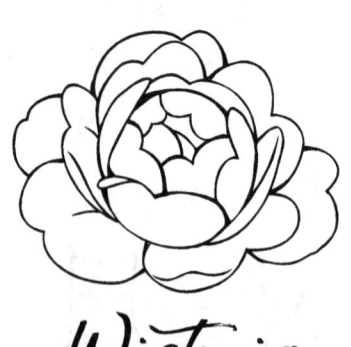

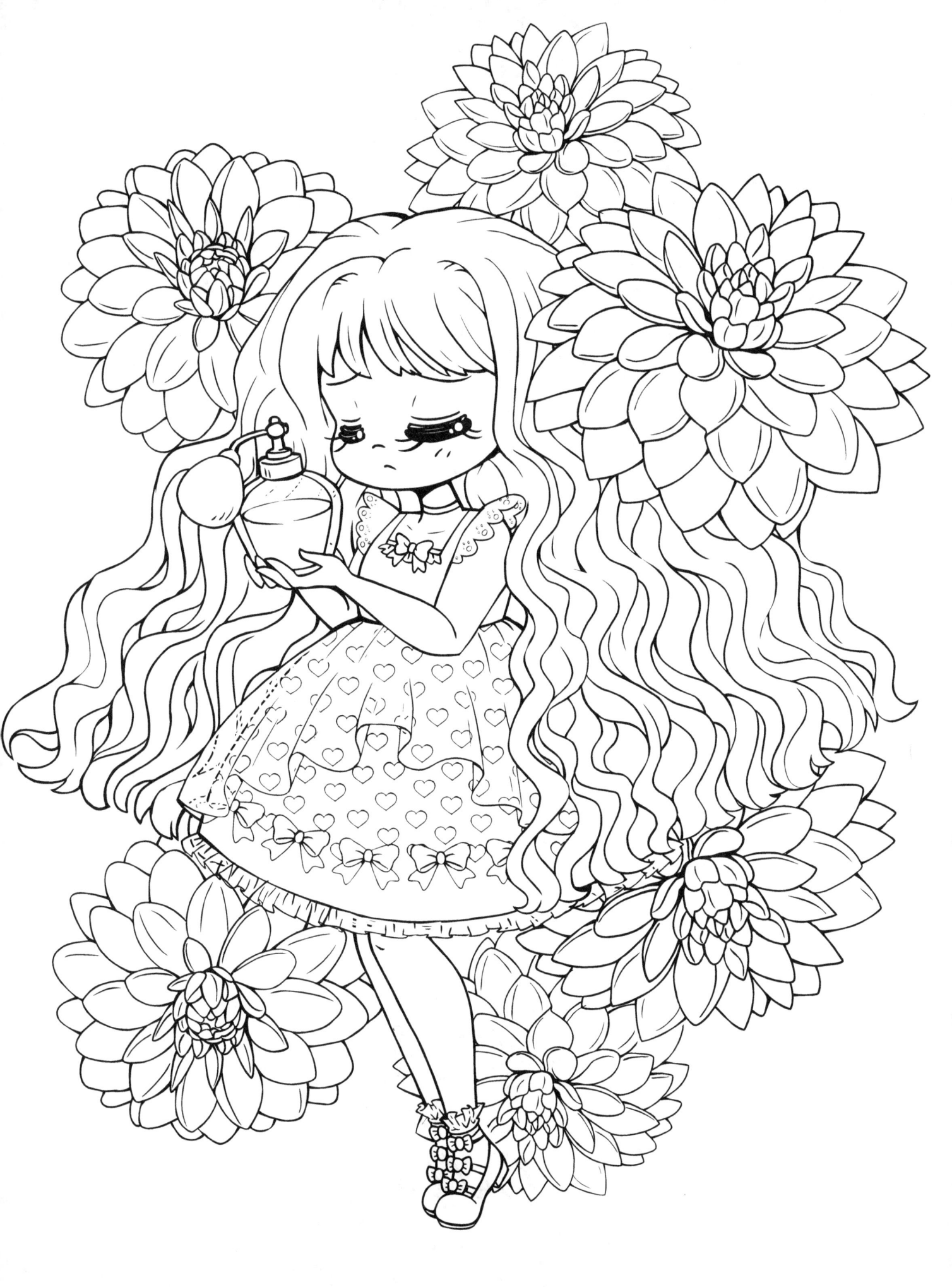

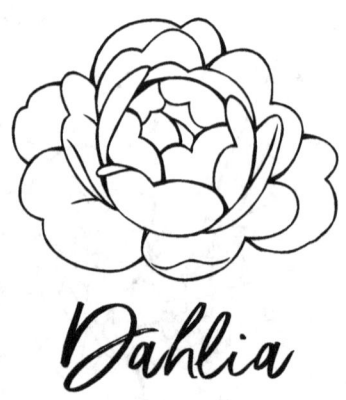

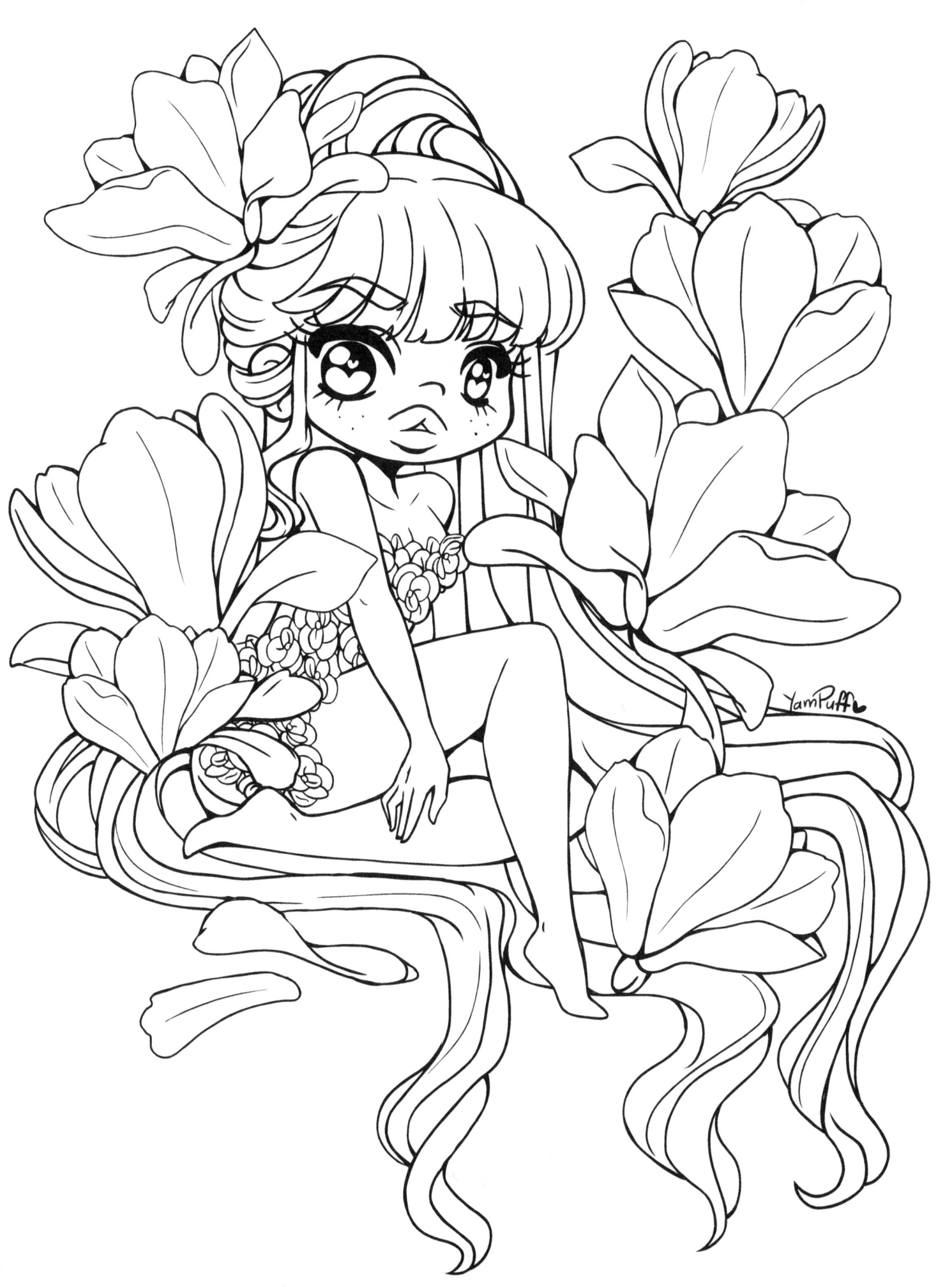

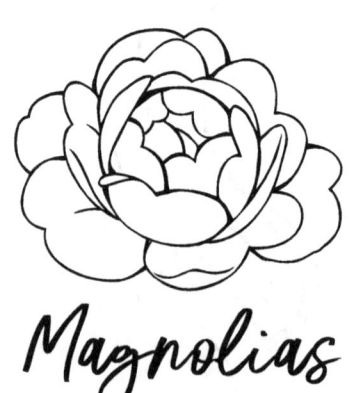

Magnolias

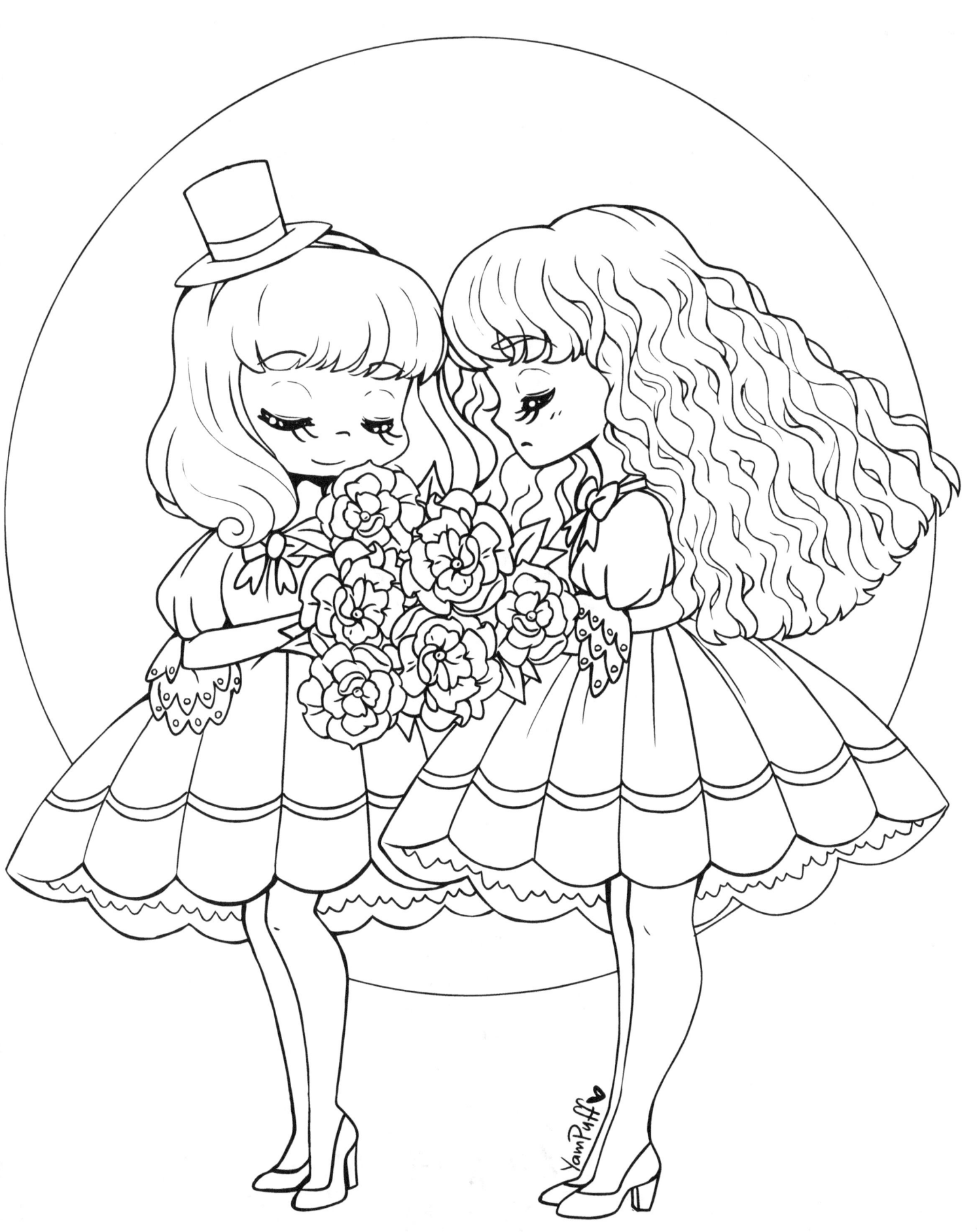

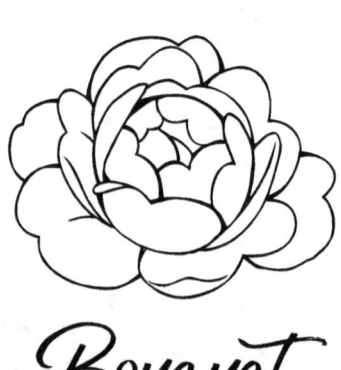

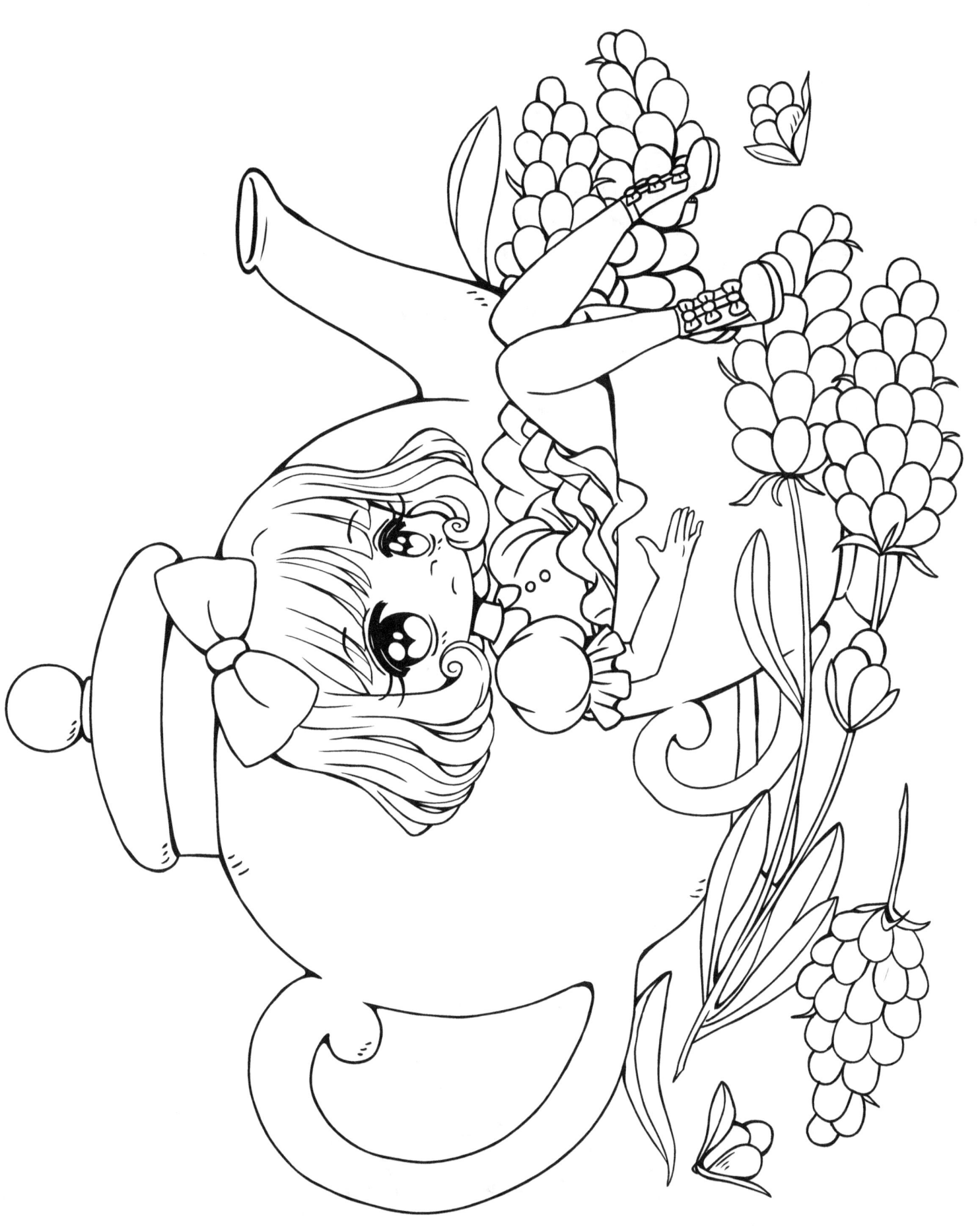

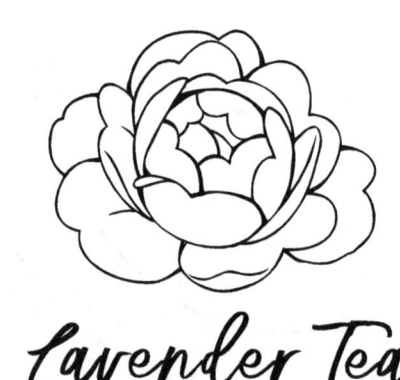

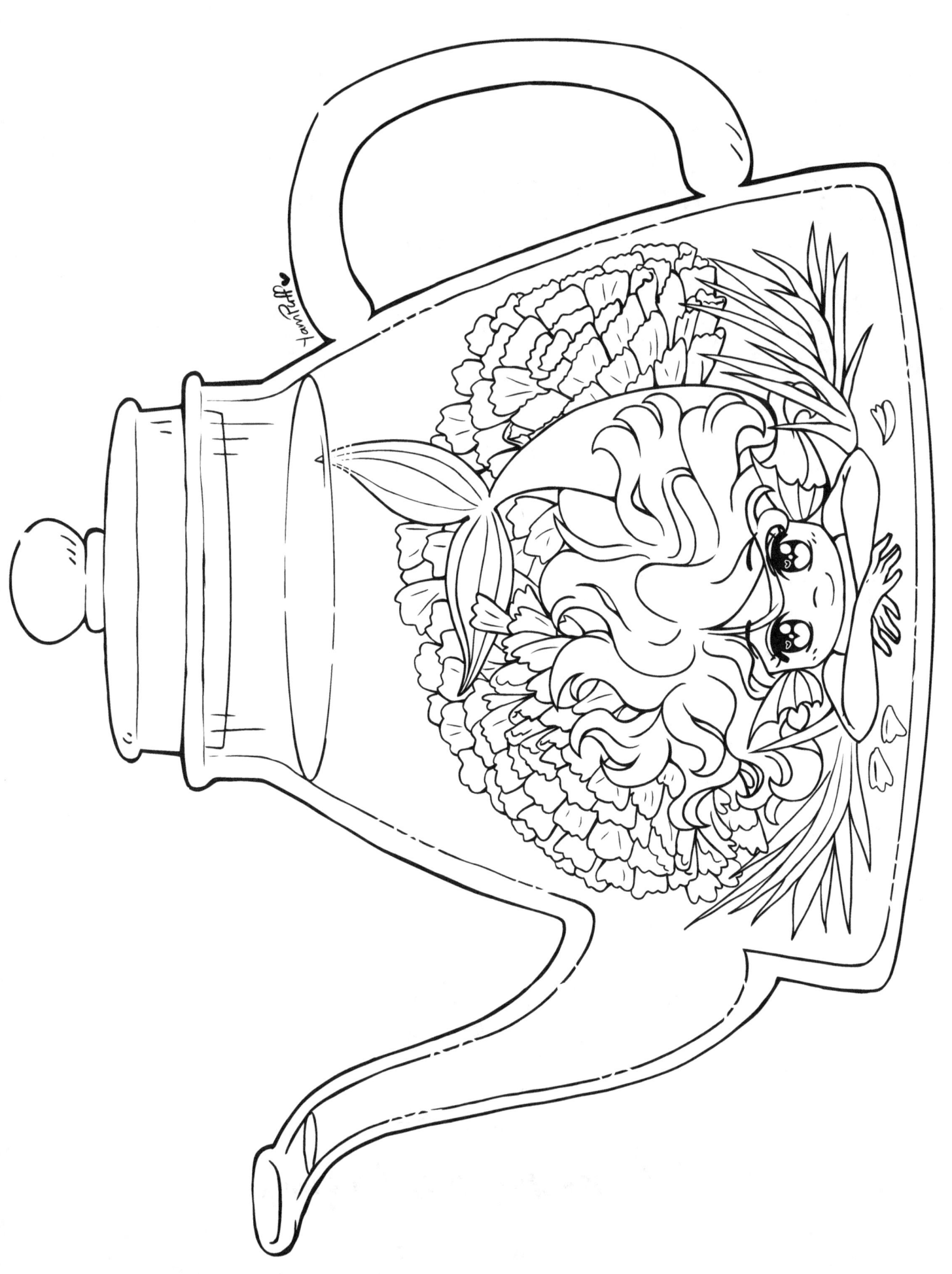

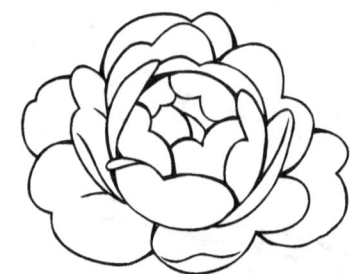

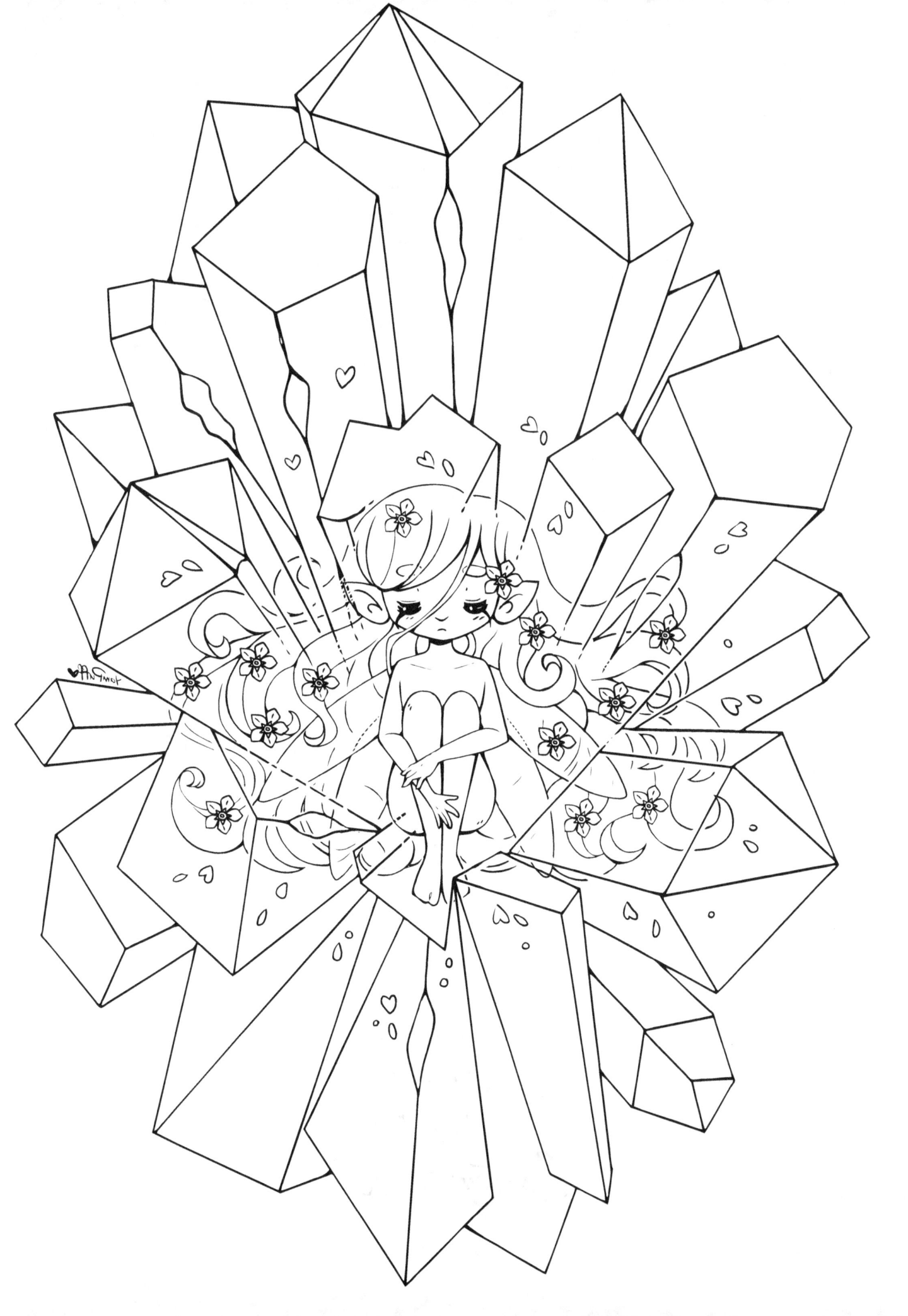

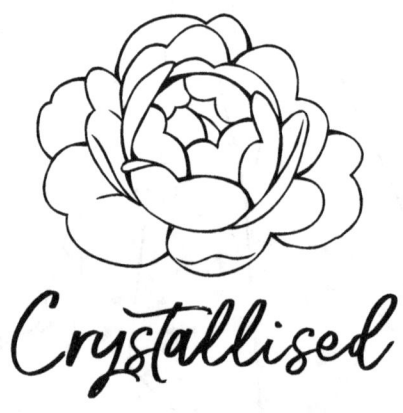

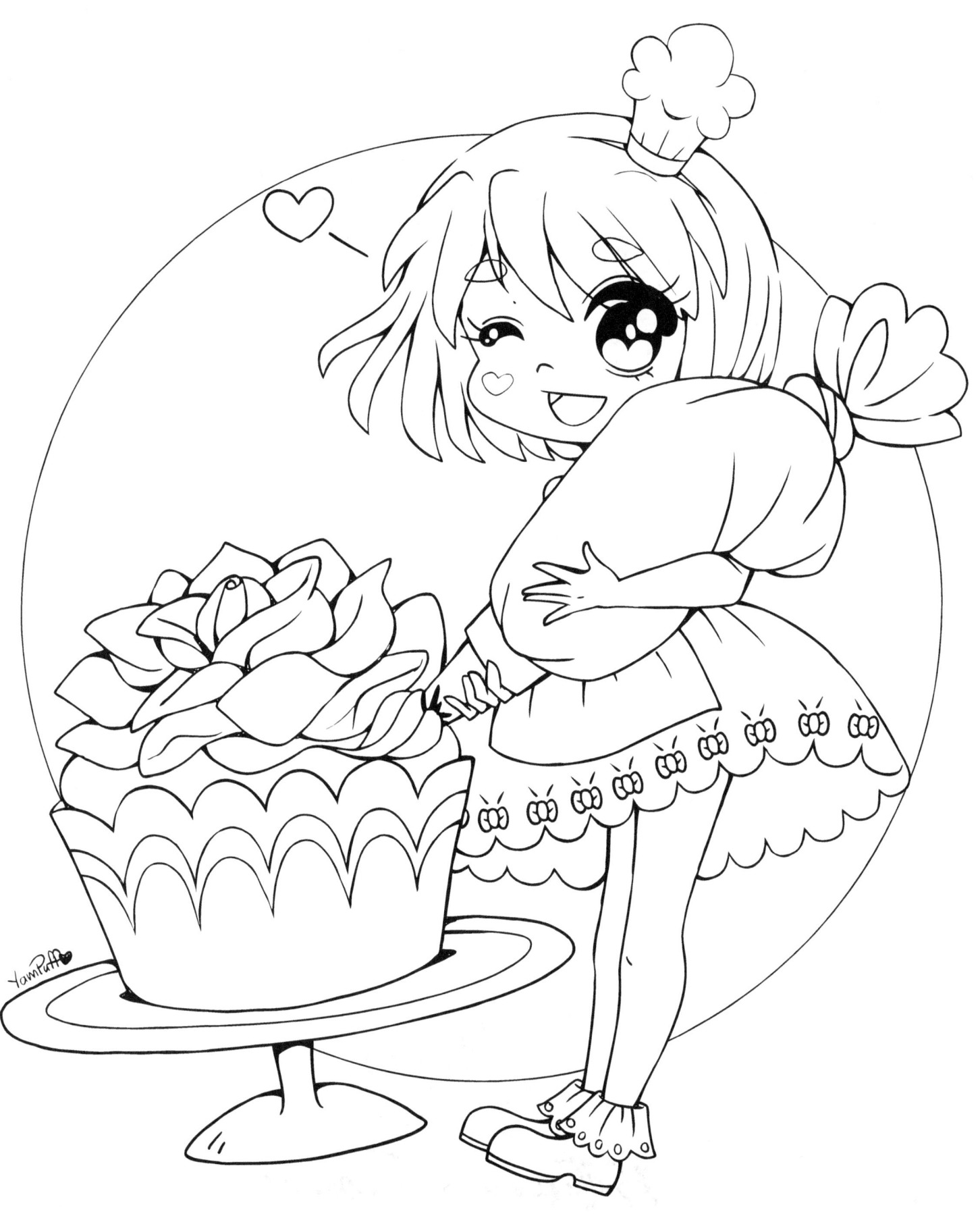

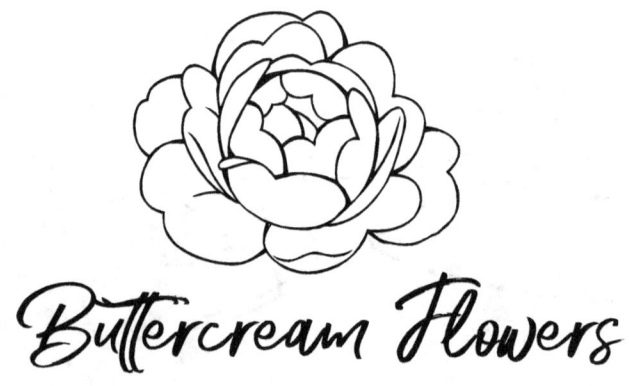

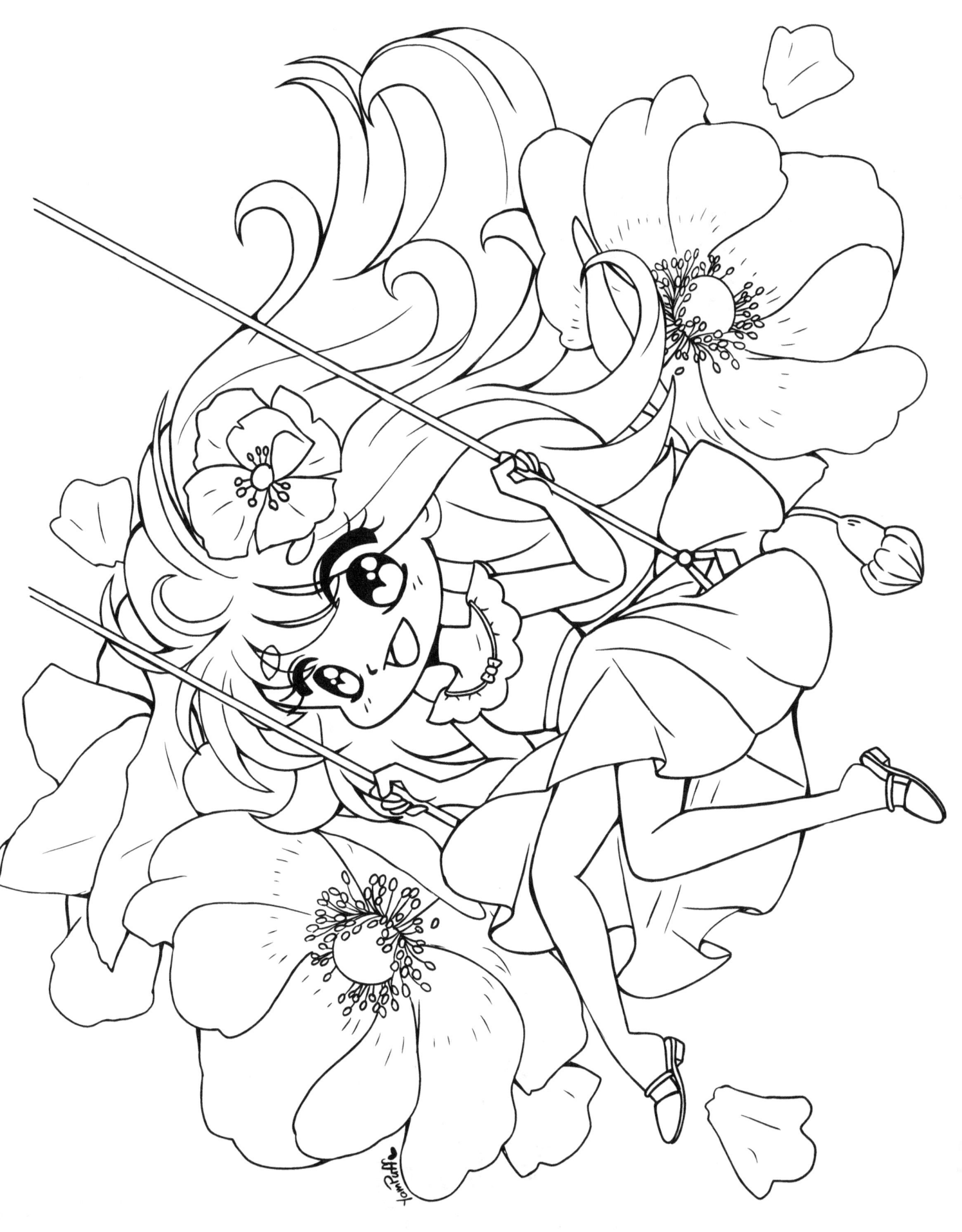

The Swing

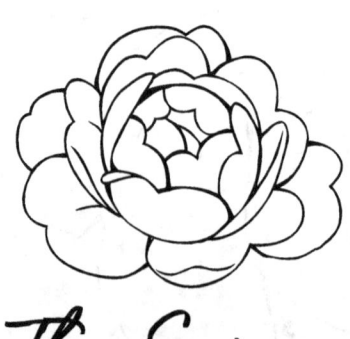

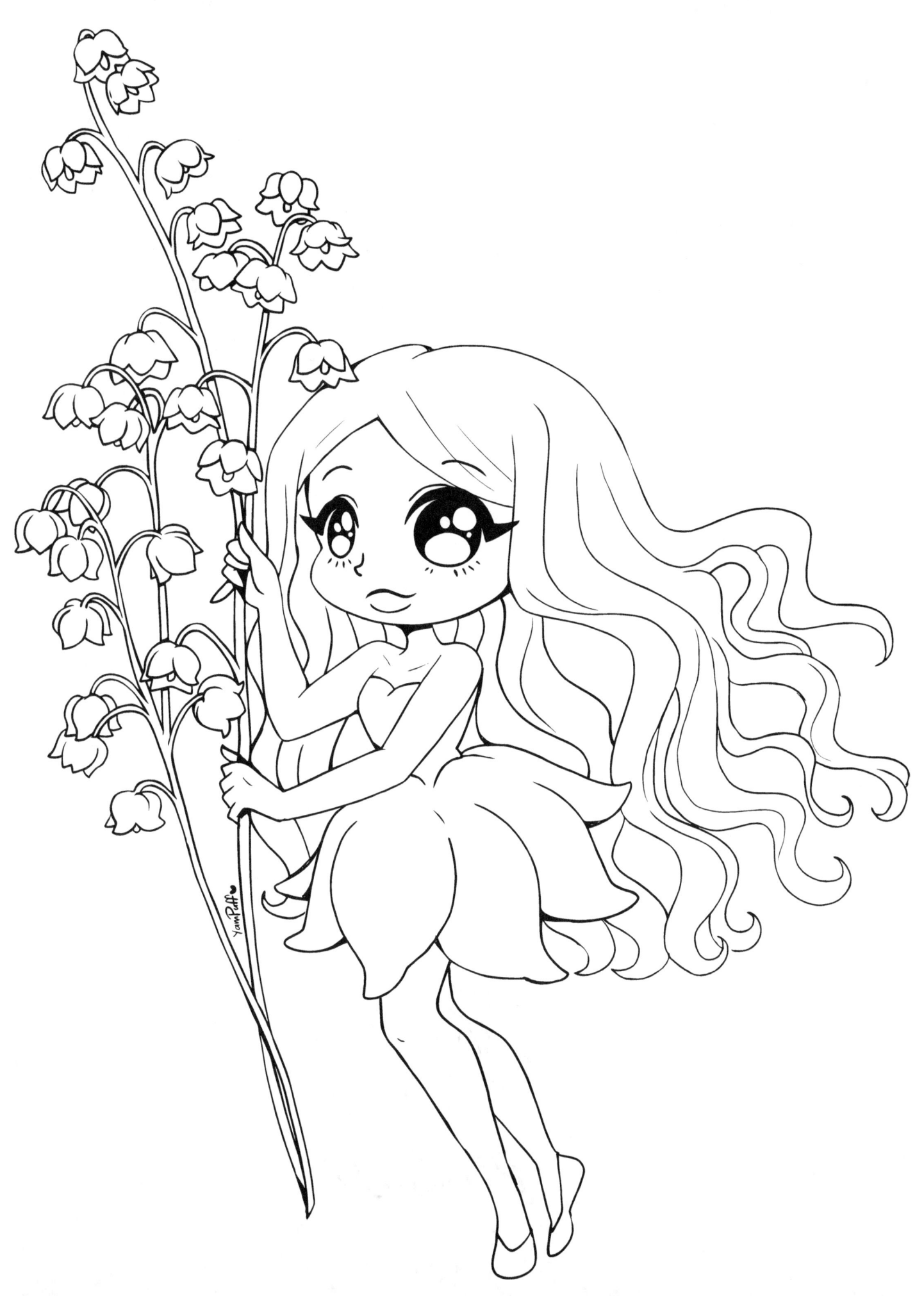

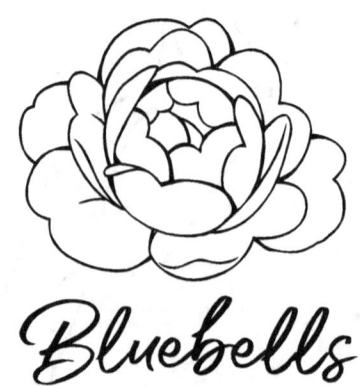

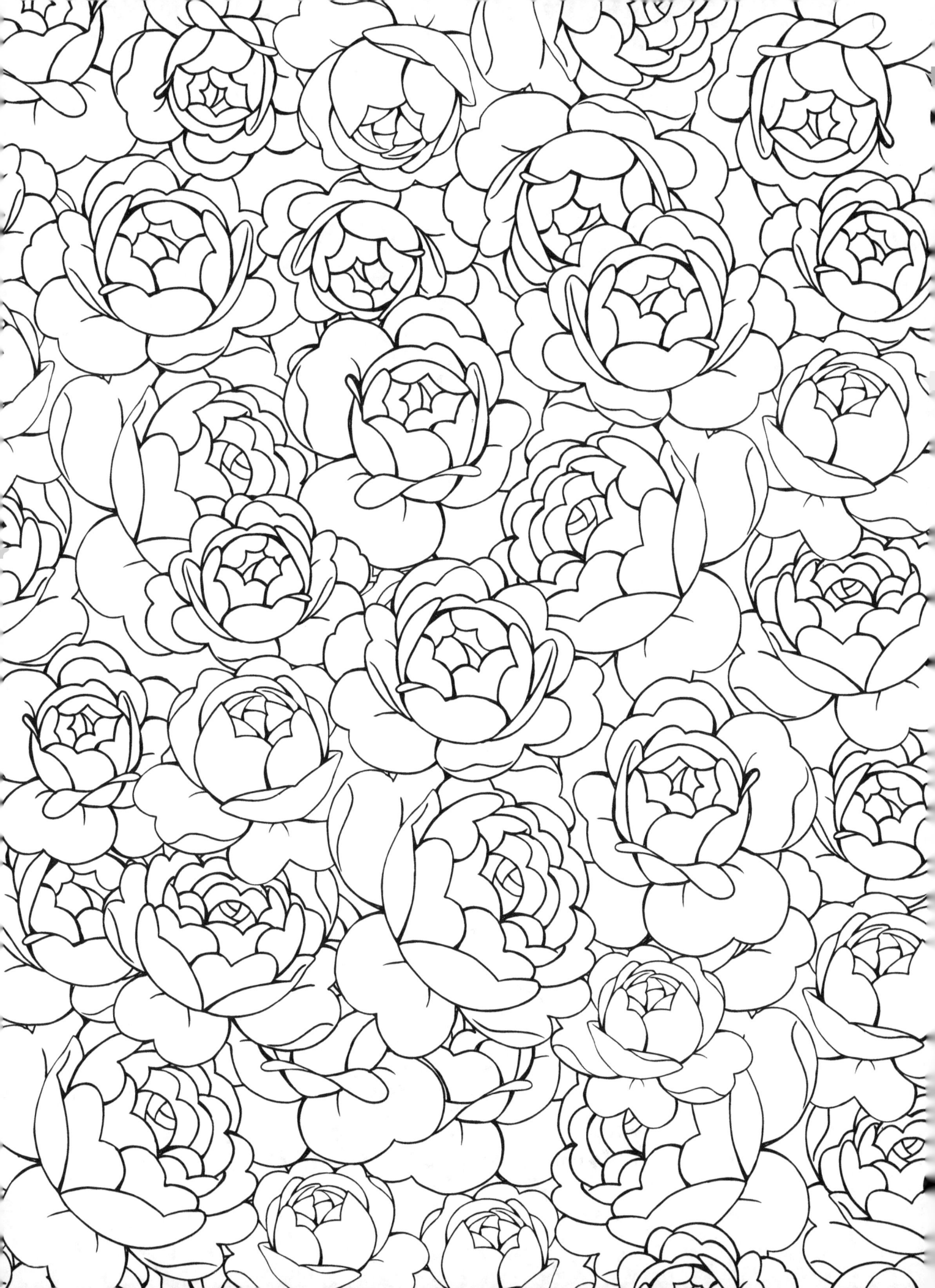

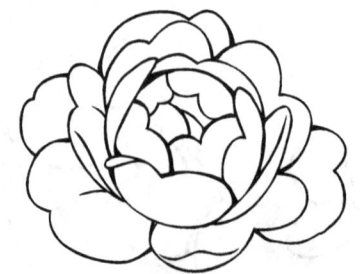

Thank you for coloring!

USE THIS PAGE TO CHECK HOW YOUR COLORS LOOK ON THE PAPER!

WANT MORE? CHECK OUT "COLOR CHARTS" BY YAMPUFF AVAILABLE ON AMAZON!

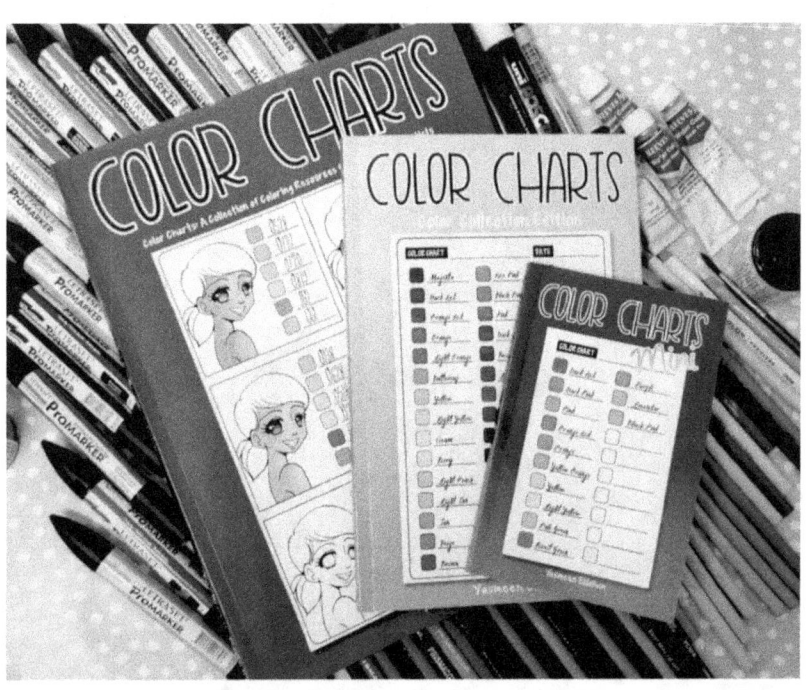

Other coloring booogks by YamPuff
available on Amazon and @ etsy.com/shop/yampuffsstuff

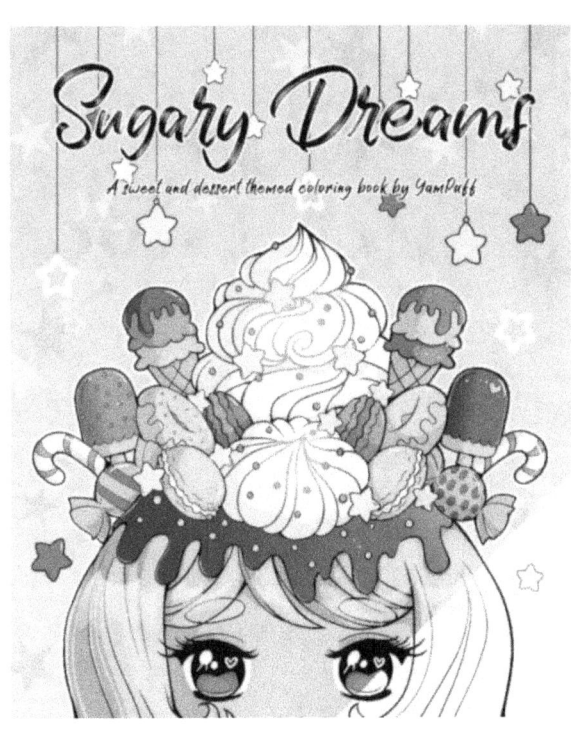

Sugary Dreams

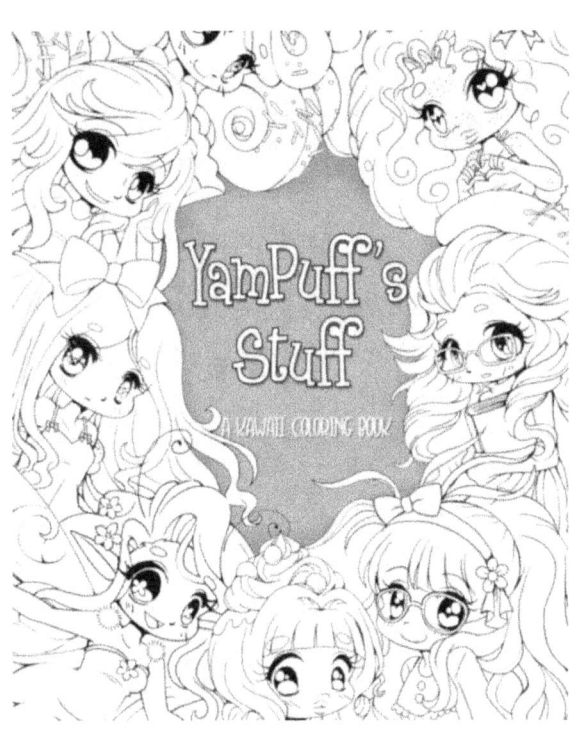

YamPuff's Stuff

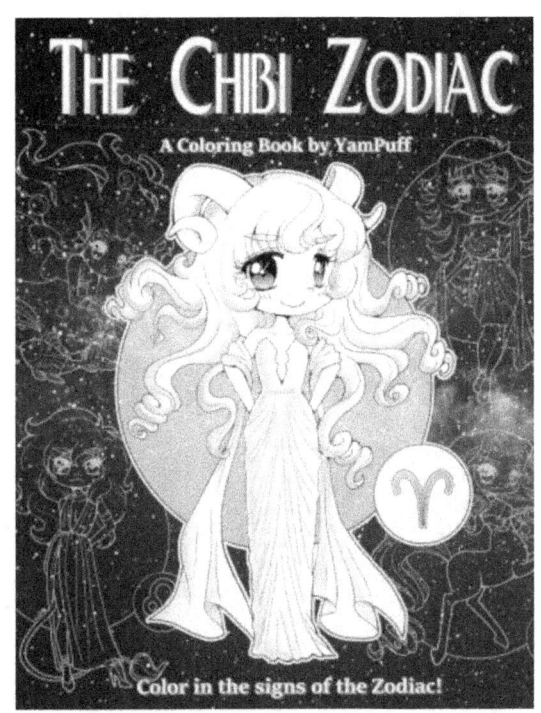

The Chibi Zodiac

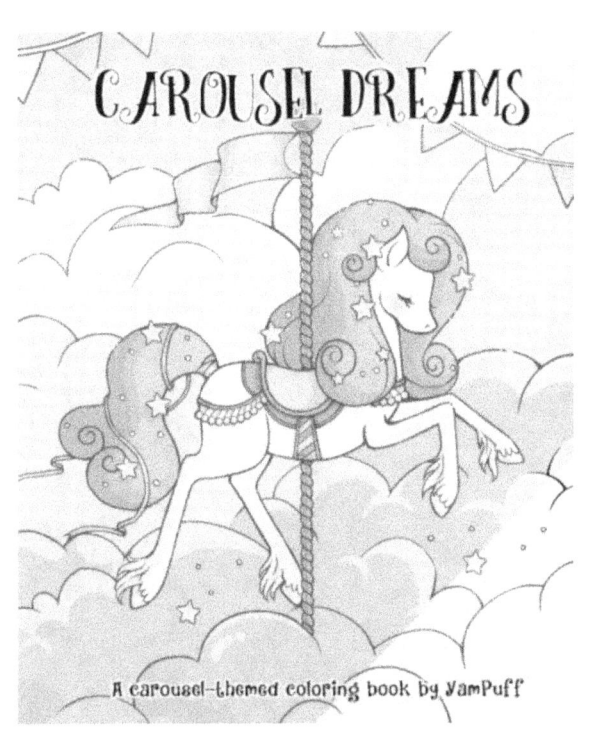

Carousel Dreams

www.ingramcontent.com/pod-product-compliance
Lightning Source LLC
Chambersburg PA
CBHW080526220526
45465CB00006B/2612